①

AMERICAN

HERITAGE

February 1958 · Volume IX, Number 2

THE SPIRIT OF THE UNION.

In 1860, as the threat of Civil War intensified northern patriotism, Currier & Ives published a series of lithographs of all the Presidents. Those of the first five, based on Gilbert Stuart portraits, are most highly prized by modern collectors. This is one of over fifty prints on George Washington, by far the most popular subject.

AMERICAN HERITAGE

The Magazine of History

PUBLISHER
James Parton

EDITORIAL DIRECTOR
Joseph J. Thorndike, Jr.

EDITOR
Bruce Catton

MANAGING EDITOR
Oliver Jensen

ASSOCIATE EDITORS
Richard M. Ketchum
Joan Paterson Mills

ASSISTANT EDITOR
Robert L. Reynolds

EDITORIAL ASSISTANTS
Hilde Heun, Stephen W. Sears
Caroline Backlund, Lilyan Goldman
Helen M. Brown, Robert Cowley
Art: Murray Belsky, Trudy Glucksberg

ART DIRECTOR
Irwin Glusker

ADVISORY BOARD
Allan Nevins, *Chairman*
Carl Carmer   Richard P. McCormick
Albert B. Corey   Harry Shaw Newman
Christopher Crittenden   Howard H. Peckham
Marshall Davidson   S. K. Stevens
Louis C. Jones   Arthur M. Schlesinger, Sr.

REGIONAL EDITORS
Ray A. Billington.........*Evanston, Illinois*
John W. Caughey....*Los Angeles, California*
K. Ross Toole............*Helena, Montana*
Walter Prescott Webb........*Austin, Texas*

STAFF PHOTOGRAPHER
Herbert Loebel

CIRCULATION DIRECTOR
Richard V. Benson

AMERICAN HERITAGE is published every two months by American Heritage Publishing Co., Inc., 551 Fifth Avenue, New York 17, N. Y.

Single Copies: $2.95
Annual Subscriptions: $12.50 in the U.S.A.
$13.50 elsewhere

An annual Index of AMERICAN HERITAGE is published every February, priced at $1.00. AMERICAN HERITAGE is also indexed in *Readers' Guide to Periodical Literature.*

AMERICAN HERITAGE will consider but assumes no responsibility for unsolicited material.

Sponsored by

American Association for State & Local History · Society of American Historians

CONTENTS *February, 1958 · Volume IX, Number 2*

COVER: These exquisite miniatures by the great Edward Greene Malbone, reproduced through the courtesy of the Carolina Art Association, not only suggest the charm of the enchanting old city of Charleston (see page 48) but recall a fragment of romance. Young Thomas Pinckney, 22, son of the Revolutionary general, was courting lovely Elizabeth Izard, 18. The scene: plays, dances, her house, and especially Malbone's studio. Like most young men, he suffered alternating agonies of jealousy, despair, and joy and at last, despite the pessimism revealed in his letters, won the girl in 1803. They lived out peaceful lives between Charleston's two great wars, less distinguished than those of their martial ancestors and descendants but perhaps happier. *Back Cover*: This old cutout belongs to the Bettman Archive.

The Yankee and the Czar

Amid the intrigue of the Russian court, John Quincy Adams took walks

with Alexander I, spoke up for America, and scored a diplomatic triumph

St. Petersburg looked like this in 1809, when Adams landed at the quay on the Neva before a statue of Peter the Great. His political career at its nadir, Adams saw his Russian assignment as "honorable diplomatic exile," but in 1825, partly as a result of this and other successes abroad, he was President. In the portrait at left the head was done by Gilbert Stuart, the body added by Thomas Sully after Stuart's death.

In late October the sun hangs low in the south over the Gulf of Finland and sets early into the Baltic's leaden waters. The equinox is usually seen only through clouds scudding from the rime-crusted shores, and it signifies not the turning point of autumn but the onset of winter, bringing ice that soon seals the harbors.

Captain Beckford of the American merchant brig *Horace,* over seventy days out of Boston, had been anxious about making Kronstadt before the ice closed in as he beat up the Baltic in the equinoctial weather of 1809. He had set out on a hot noon in early August from the wharf of his owner, William Gray, just as the Boston and Charlestown bells rang the hour. Aboard he had a cargo of American and West Indian staples such as cotton, tobacco, sugar, and coffee to be traded for Russian hemp, cordage, iron, and naval stores. He also carried a distinguished passenger, a friend of owner

Gray, going abroad on an official diplomatic mission.

Europe was at war, as it had been off and on for over fifteen years. The *Horace*'s passage was delayed, once she entered the North Sea, by the British on one hand and the allies of Napoleon on the other—two sides each blockading the other and thereby harrying neutral traffic. After being boarded by two of the King's ships and then hailed into a port of the opposing Danes, Captain Beckford thought he had best give up trying to reach Kronstadt before winter and lay over in Germany until the spring. But his passenger, a prematurely bald man just over forty, with an air of austerity that sometimes relaxed after a glass of wine at the Captain's table, called on him to push on despite the obstacles.

So on October 22 the *Horace* finally made landfall on the gray headlands of Kronstadt, entry port of imperial Russia's vast domain. A guard ship drew near.

By WILLIAM HARLAN HALE

The *Horace* asked for a pilot, but a three-hour wait in the blustery roadstead produced none. By now it was dusk, and the passenger hailed the guard ship for a boat to take him ashore for overnight lodgings. On the way in he was challenged by a naval barge and summoned by officers speaking German to present himself to the commandant of the port, one Admiral Kolokoltzof. This the visitor did, and on landing introduced himself as John Quincy Adams, Minister Plenipotentiary of the United States of America to the Court of His Imperial Majesty Alexander, Czar and Autocrat of All the Russias.

Therewith began one of the most remarkable missions in the history of American diplomacy, as well as one of its most engaging ones. The crusty son of rugged John Adams, reared to be the leading young Puritan of Boston, found himself as America's first plenipotentiary at the most extravagant, Byzantine, and corrupt court of Europe.* His four years there were ones of rising tumult and drama, during which the envoy of the faraway republic conducted himself with an aplomb that captivated the most cynical of

---

* The United States had had consular representation in Russia since 1794, and in 1808 President Jefferson had appointed a minister to St. Petersburg, but a Senate dubious of foreign inveiglements and of Russia in particular had refused to confirm him.

courtiers and a success that astonished even himself.

He walked with Alexander I when the youthful Czar and the conquering Napoleon were at the height of their exuberant friendship, having just divided between them virtually all the continent of Europe. He saw that friendship break up and end in Napoleon's suicidal march on Moscow—and was in fact himself, like some fateful herald in classic tragedy, a contributor to that outcome. He not only observed the struggle of the dynasts at close range, but he spoke up on every side for our own American rights and aims and did so in such a way as to bring home what his historian grandson, Henry Adams (naturally disposed to favor the Adamses), called a diplomatic triumph "Napoleonic in its magnitude." And amid all this he enjoyed himself in this exotic environment, dining out among the titled great, seeing the dawn in at balls, and even being captivated by the voracious Mme de Staël, the greatest man-killer of her day, although on mornings after he sometimes wrote self-reproving entries in his diary about "this life of dissipation."

Admiral Kolokoltzof showed every courtesy to the visitor on learning who he was and offered him and Mrs. Adams (accompanied by little Charles Francis Adams, then aged two) a government barge to take them up the river Neva next day to St. Petersburg.

Tacking up the narrow channel past palaces and swamps, they drew up at length at the city quay opposite the huge equestrian statue that the late Empress Catherine had erected to her predecessor, Peter the Great, builder of this baroque metropolis on its twilit northern marshland.

Remote as the scene was from his house in Boylston Street, Adams was no stranger to it. He had in fact lived here for over a year when he was a schoolboy and America was not yet a republic. He had seen the great Empress Catherine in her splendor. Precocious in all things, Adams was never more so than when he had come here in 1781 directly from school to serve as private secretary to Francis Dana, an agent sent out by the Continental Congress in the vague hope of aid from Russia. Dana could speak no word of French, the language of the Russian court, and so John Adams had lent him his own son, who could speak it with ease and who thus became a diplomatic interpreter at fourteen. Almost thirty years later, at the table of the Russian imperial chancellor, Minister Adams caused surprise when he recalled that he had dined in this very house in company with the then French minister over half a generation before.

Schooled abroad also while accompanying his father on special missions, young Adams had come into his own diplomat's estate as envoy to Holland at twenty-seven and to Prussia at thirty—altogether a preparation unique in our annals. Yet The Hague and Berlin at that time were hardly to be compared with glittering St. Petersburg, now the hub of half of Europe. Here, far down on the list, Adams found himself amid a high-titled, high-living diplomatic corps that included such names as Count Schenk de Castel Deschingen, minister of Würtemberg; the Duc de Mondragone, minister of the kingdom of Naples; General Pardo de Figueroa, minister of Spain; Baron de Bussche Hunnefeldt, minister of Westphalia; Count de Maistre, minister of Sardinia; and, leading all the rest, the magnificent figure of Armand Augustin Louis de Caulaincourt, Duc de Vicence, Master of the Horse to His Majesty the Emperor Napoleon, and ambassador of France.

Still, minor as the American seemed in this company, high Russian officialdom promptly welcomed him. Within five days of his arrival Adams found himself at his first diplomatic dinner at the home of the chancellor, rotund, oleaginous Count Romanzoff, in

In St. Petersburg Adams often witnessed parades of Russian troops before the Imperial Palace. He shared the capital's excitement as, aided by "General Winter," the Czar's soldiers chased Napoleon's beaten armies across the snows.

Adams' companion in promenades along the Neva was the young and charming Czar Alexander I. Adams described him as "the Titus of the Age, the Delight of Human Kind."

company with the dashing Caulaincourt himself. Over forty sat down at table in what Adams described as "the style of highest splendor," the men being "covered with stars and ribbons beyond anything that I had ever seen"—and he had seen Paris and London as well. The Chancellor took him aside to show him superb Sèvres vases presented to him personally by Napoleon—a hint, if any was needed, of the close relations between the two capitals. And the mood that night was one of special festivity. News had just come in that Russia's ally Napoleon had signed a new, victorious peace with Austria following his triumph on the field of Wagram.

Within another week the American minister was received by the Czar, also under circumstances that suggested favor. Protocol specified that an arriving envoy, after being escorted through the succession of antechambers of the Imperial Palace, enter the Czar's private cabinet with three deep bows, there to be presented by the master of ceremonies to the monarch standing in mid-room, after which a set address was to be delivered to accompany submission of the letter of credence. Yet Adams had barely begun upon his bows when Czar Alexander, alone in his room, advanced on him and disarmingly greeted him: "Monsieur, je suis charmé d'avoir le plaisir de vous voir ici."

This was sometimes Alexander's way. Far from being forbidding, he was at the time Adams met him the most ingratiating, the most handsome, and also the most tantalizing monarch of Europe. Then 32, tall, majestic, and already growing stout, he both looked and acted younger than his years. His complexion was strangely delicate; his eyes were almost boyishly bright; he wore his golden blond hair arranged in imitation of the heads on antique medallions. When he spoke, his voice adapted itself to each visitor, passing through myriads of shadings designed to convey friendly sentiment and solicitude. He enthused about French philosophy, Rousseau, even American republicanism, and was hard to pin down on anything. He looked the part of a young god, yet everyone knew that his late father had been insane and had been murdered in his own palace by Alexander's friends. Napoleon, baffled, called him "The Northern Sphinx." Adams, the junior minister at court, resolved to draw him out.

Their first meeting began with the usual exchange of amenities, Adams voicing on behalf of President Madison the hope that this mission would further the ties of friendship and commerce between the two countries and the Czar reciprocating with like sentiments. America's position toward the "disturbances" presently agitating Europe, Alexander went on to say, was "wise and just." He turned to the latest disturbance, namely, his own current war with Britain, and remarked, "The only obstacle to a general pacification of Europe is the obstinate adherence of England to a system of maritime pretensions which is neither liberal nor just. The only object of the war now is to bring England to reasonable terms on this subject."

To Adams, apostle of the American doctrine of freedom of the seas, these were welcome words. The Czar took him by the arm and led him to the window overlooking the Neva. "As for me, I shall adhere invariably to those [principles] which I have declared"—meaning those he had declared to Adams about the rights of neutral navigation in time of war, although he hadn't clearly declared them before. Adams at once remarked that the President would be highly gratified to find his Imperial Majesty in such agreement with our own American position, particularly since our country was "a great commercial and pacific nation." The United States, he added succinctly, would use all means in its power consistent with peace and its separation from Europe "to contribute to the support of the liberal principles to which your Majesty has expressed so strong and so just an attachment."

The talk continued far beyond the time usually allotted for presentations, ranging over topics from the climate of Massachusetts to the geographic extent of Russia. "Its size is one of its greatest evils," the Czar mused of his own country. "It is difficult to hold together so great a body as this empire."

Adams had reason to be gratified by his first interview with the Czar. As his dispatches to the State Department show, he was aware of the strong impression he himself had made. What he did not know at the time was that there was another reason for the Czar's special cordiality. On the very day of their interview, Alexander was privately weighing a move that was to become fateful for him, for Napoleon, and for all Europe.

The young Czar was fighting Britain and her pretensions on the seas. Yet his bosom French ally was never more triumphant than now after his newest victory over Austria, and the peace he had imposed on her—in which France crept still closer to Russia's borders—showed little consideration for the Czar's aid and loyalty. Moreover, through his Continental System of counterblockade against England, Napoleon had set *himself* up as arbiter of all that moved to and from Europe by water, including that which moved to Russia. So the Czar found it interesting just now to talk at length to this short, well-spoken visitor from a neutral, transatlantic country that seemed to have no interest but peaceable trade. Very interesting, in fact. Who knew, in the end. . . .

Two days later, Alexander made his first move against his French friend. It was only a gesture—an expression of complaint at some of the terms of Napoleon's Austrian treaty, cast in the flowery, courtly language of friendship—yet it cast its shadow before. From here the paths of the emperors began, at first imperceptibly, to part. It was Adams' fortune to be present at the right place at a moment of historic change and to expound ideas that found echo in the mind of Napoleon's uneasy partner in the game of European grab.

Adams' own object was by no means to breed dissension among monarchs. It was simply to stop their interference with American shipping in the Baltic—a problem most acute in the narrow seas controlled by Denmark under Napoleonic edicts. But when he first raised the matter with Romanzoff, the pro-French chancellor sighed, saying that of course it would be pleasant if allied Denmark became more "liberal," but that under present circumstances "this is a dream."

Down these "ice-hills," which resemble American ski jumps of a later day, slid the dignified Adams and other foreign diplomats, without benefit of sled or toboggan. In the background are the towers of St. Petersburg.

Meanwhile the affairs of Europe moved at their slow, measured pace. It took a courier two weeks in winter to get through from Paris to the Russian capital, while Adams was fortunate if he could get an answer to a dispatch of his to Washington within six months. So there was time to look about, observe, and even amuse oneself.

Within less than a week of his arrival he had done some systematic sampling of Russian liquors—particularly the heady *kvass* and *chitslitsky*, which he found tasted like "small beer." He found them "not unpalatable," although Mrs. Adams didn't agree. Then he attended his first full-dress royal affair, a *Te Deum* sung at the palace chapel in honor of the new Austro-French peace, beginning with a salute of cannon from the Admiralty and continuing for two hours as candles and icons were borne in procession and the Czar kissed the crucifix proffered him by the Archbishop.

Next came a ball at Chancellor Romanzoff's, lasting very late, at which again "the dresses were more splendid, and the profusion of diamonds and other precious stones worn by both the men and women . . . was greater than I ever witnessed anywhere." There the empress mother, widow of the late mad, assassinated czar, conversed at length with Adams on the subject of the St. Petersburg weather, which in November was notoriously bad.

This was followed by a dinner given by Count Einsiedel, the minister of Saxony, at which Adams shone by discussing German literature with his host, Homer with the Spanish minister, and the new constitution of Holland with the Dutch envoy. Next came a gala affair at the French ambassador's, at which forty sat down to dinner and then heard Mlle Bourgoin, an actress imported from Paris, declaim scenes from Racine's *Phèdre*. Afterward dancing began with a polonaise, while a French jester performed sleight-of-hand tricks

CONTINUED ON PAGE 82

9

"*The President came forward and*

The winter of 1864–65 had been unusually cold, with ice on the Potomac so thick that it could support crowds of skaters who were in a gay mood despite the war. But in Petersburg and Richmond, where the war was very real, the remnants of Lee's Army of Northern Virginia clung grimly to the elaborate network of fortifications and trenches that guarded the two cities. Only a few hundred yards away, their Union counterparts opposed the Confederate lines. The two armies had been locked together since the previous summer, when Grant had begun his siege. Fighting had never stopped, but action had slowed down considerably while the soldiers huddled in their dugouts for warmth. Farther south, Sherman's victorious army had swept through Georgia and South Carolina and was moving into North Carolina with Goldsboro as its immediate goal.

On March 4 it had been raining for two days all through the East. In Washington the rain had come down in torrents at daybreak and then had let up, so that by half-past ten the enormous crowds, which had flocked to the city to see the

By PHILIP VAN DOREN STERN

the sun burst through the clouds"

second inauguration of their wartime President, ventured hopefully into the streets. People kept looking anxiously at the sky, for rain at noon would mean that the President would have to take his oath of office inside the Capitol, where only the favored few who held tickets could witness the ceremony. Ten minutes later it began to rain again. Hardy blue-coated veterans, who were used to being soaked to the skin for days, watched scornfully while civilians and their women fled to shelter. But the crowds were so dense that it took time to clear the streets, and many got drenched in the sudden downpour.

Even worse than the rain, though, was the mud. The New York *Herald*'s correspondent said of it: "There is mud in Pennsylvania Avenue and all the other avenues. . . . The streets are flooded and afloat with a vile yellow fluid, not thick enough to walk on nor thin enough to swim in. This yellow material added to the holiday appearance of the people, marking them with gay and festive spots from head to heel. All the backs were yellow with it, and all the

Frank Leslie's Illustrated Newspaper, 1865

horses, and all the little boys—all the world floundered about in it, and swore at it, and laughed at it. In Pennsylvania Avenue it was not so deep as in many other places, for as that street was paved, it was possible to touch bottom there. It was blacker there, however . . . and when it spattered on people it did not look so much like golden spangles."

The President was already at the Capitol, signing last-minute bills before the Thirty-eighth Congress adjourned at noon. In Lafayette Square and in the grounds around the White House there was a great deal of stirring about as soldiers, marshals, volunteer firemen, and civilians got ready to take their places in the grand procession up Pennsylvania Avenue to the Capitol. About eleven o'clock the procession began to form. Mrs. Lincoln got into a closed carriage; after a long delay she began to worry about being late so she ordered the coachman to go ahead and drive quickly. As her carriage hurried to the Capitol everyone took it for granted that the President was inside, and the crowd cheered him *in absentia* all along the way.

Mrs. Lincoln's haste upset the carefully planned arrangements for the procession, but at last it began to move. The bells of the city rang out, military bands played lustily, and on one of the floats, a miniature replica of the *Monitor*, sailors fired blank charges from the cannon in the turret. Another float, which advertised the Washington *Daily Chronicle*, had a printing press in full operation, with handbills being tossed to the crowd as fast as they were printed. The uncertain weather had spoiled the effect which a float carrying a Temple of Liberty was expected to achieve. The pretty girls in white dresses who were supposed to grace the temple refused to risk their costumes on such an undependable day, and their places were taken by badly behaved small boys who made a lark out of what was intended as a dignified display. But the visiting firemen from Philadelphia and their Washington hosts put on an impressive show as their beautifully decorated and shined-up engines moved along the muddy street. And, for the first time in the history of Washington, two companies of Negro troops and a Lodge of Negro Odd Fellows in full regalia took part in an inauguration parade.

The Thirty-eighth Congress had worked all night to finish the final business of the session, while the President and his Cabinet had stayed at the Capitol on the evening of March 3 until after midnight. When members left the House and Senate chambers early in the morning of March 4, they found that people who had not been able to get accommodations in the overcrowded city were sleeping in the Capitol. It was raining so hard that no one had the heart to turn them

out, even though the building soon had to be cleared for the ceremonies of the day.

The President had returned and was in the ornately decorated room set aside for him in the Senate wing, so busy reading bills that he had not thought to remove his tall hat. He sat there all morning with it on, reading the bills and

These medallions appeared

affixing the signature "A. Lincoln" to those he wanted to approve. (One of the bills he signed in the closing days of the Thirty-eighth Congress was for extra pensions for the last five survivors of the American Revolution.) Senators Foster and Hendricks were with the President, while pages kept running in and out of the room. They heard the inaugural procession reach the Capitol; then they heard the footsteps and subdued murmurs of many people crowding through the halls.

The President was due to appear in the Senate chamber at noon, but when noon came the Senate was not yet ready for him. One of the pages told the men in the little room that Vice President-elect An-

This rare photograph shows troops and spectators gathering
fore the Capitol for the inauguration. A reporter estimated th

tations to the Inaugural Ball.

drew Johnson was speaking longer than had been expected. The people around the President grew more and more impatient. They sent a marshal to make sure that Chief Justice Salmon P. Chase was on hand; then they escorted the President down the hall to the Senate chamber.

Johnson was still speaking when the presidential party entered the Senate chamber. His face was red and his voice boomed above all the rustle and bustle of the densely crowded room. When President Lincoln unobtrusively took his seat at the end of the clerk's desk, there was audible whispering from the ladies in the galleries, and there was much craning of necks while comment buzzed everywhere. Johnson spoke even more loudly in order to be heard, and then, as the noise died away, his voice was left stranded on a peak of sound.

Johnson was a stump speaker who could rouse a backwoods audience. He had been the war governor of Tennessee and had had much more experience in Washington in both the House and the Senate than

y the time Lincoln appeared the crowd had swelled to over 30,000, despite the depth of mud in which they were obliged to stand."

Lincoln. But he had few friends in the Capitol; his uncertain political position as a lifelong Democrat who consented to be elected to office with a Republican President on the Union ticket had made him distrusted and unpopular.

Lincoln had outgrown his log-cabin background, but Johnson was still suffering from a poor-boy complex. He liked to boast of his lowly origin, of being a tailor by trade and a man of the people, but when he spoke, he used long words of Latin or Greek derivation to show how learned he had become. He enjoyed calling himself a plebeian. The word had caught his fancy; it was the kind of word that conjured up images of immense crowds in the Roman forum, where a white-robed speaker swayed the multitudes and through them ruled an empire. He had seized upon this word and made it his own. But the magic word was to betray him on this, the most important day of his life.

He had been seriously ill in Nashville for many weeks with a fever that was probably malarial, and he had not felt well enough to travel to Washington for the inauguration. He had even written to the chief clerk of the secretary of the Senate to find out whether it was absolutely necessary for him to be present that day and was told that six previous Vice Presidents had been sworn in months after Inauguration Day. But Lincoln had urged him to come to Washington, saying that he and several members of his Cabinet had unanimously concluded "that it is unsafe for you not to be here on the fourth of March. Be sure to reach here by that time."

Once the dutiful Johnson had decided to go to Washington, neither illness nor the very real possibility of assassination could stop him. On the morning of Inauguration Day, Senator J. R. Doolittle of Wisconsin called for him at his hotel and escorted him to the Vice President's Room in the Capitol, where he met his predecessor, Hannibal Hamlin. What happened that morning is explained in a newspaper clipping from the Boston *Commonwealth*, which was sent to Johnson by one of his admirers and which he carefully preserved for the rest of his life:

"There was nothing unusual in his [Johnson's] appearance, except that he did not seem in robust health. . . . Conversation proceeded on ordinary topics for a few minutes, when Mr. Johnson asked Mr. Hamlin if he had any liquor in the room, stating that he was sick and nervous. . . . Brandy being indicated, a bottle was brought by one of the pages. It was opened, a tumbler provided, and Mr. Johnson poured it about two-thirds full. . . . When near 12 . . . Mr. Hamlin rose, moved to the door near which the Sergeant-at-Arms stood, and suggested to Mr. Johnson

The White House reception on the evening of Inauguration Day was pictured in this 1865 lithograph from Leslie's Chimney Corner. *The artist has mistakenly included General and Mrs. Grant (shown being presented to the Lincolns), who were not present. At the President's right is Vice President Johnson, and standing in a row behind him are Chief Justice Salmon P. Chase, Secretary of War Edwin M. Stanton, Chase's daughter Kate, and Secretary of State William H. Seward.*

to come also. The latter got up and . . . said, 'Excuse me a moment,' and walked hastily back to where the bottle was deposited. Mr. Hamlin saw him . . . pour as large a quantity as before into the glass and drink it down like water. They then went into the Senate Chamber.''

The rain had made everything uncertain, because it was still an open question whether the presidential part of the great spectacle could be staged outdoors. The Vice President customarily took his oath of office in the Senate chamber, and just seven minutes had been allowed for his speech.

The big room was filling up rapidly when the Vice President-elect came in, leaning rather heavily on Hamlin's arm. The galleries were already well filled, and the ladies' section was even noisier than usual, for the stylishly dressed women seated there had no intention of allowing anyone to hush them up. Several senators had made requests for silence, but the privileged ladies who held official tickets of admission were so engrossed in their own conversation that they did not even hear what was being said on the floor.

A New York *Herald* correspondent described the scene: "A noise was heard in the diplomatic gallery. All eyes were turned in that direction. The noise that attracted attention arose from one of the representatives of a South American government getting his feet entangled with a mass of crinoline, losing his balance, and rolling down the aisle in the gallery."

Hamlin took the chair and began his farewell message to the Senate. While he was speaking, members of the Cabinet and seven of the ten justices of the Supreme Court entered the room. Chief Justice Chase was carrying a copy of the Constitution and a Bible so he could administer the oath of office to the President. Heads were turned toward the diplomatic gallery when Mrs. Lincoln appeared there. Reporters noted dutifully that she was wearing "a black velvet dress trimmed with ermine." Then representatives of various foreign governments, resplendent with medals and insignia of rank, were seated behind the justices of the Supreme Court.

Hamlin's farewell address was a short and gracious speech in which he simply thanked the senators for their kindness to him. At its conclusion he turned to

Johnson and asked him if he was ready to take the oath of office as Vice President. Johnson stood up and said that he was, but instead of waiting for Hamlin to administer the oath, he plunged abruptly into what was apparently intended to be his speech of acceptance. Only the newspaper accounts of the day give a truthful approximation of what he actually said.*

The New York *World*, an opposition paper which was to plague Johnson with his own words for weeks afterward, reported the speech as follows: "By choice of the people, he said, he had been made presiding officer of this body, and, in presenting himself here in obedience to the behests of the Constitution of the United States, it would, perhaps, not be out of place to remark just here what a striking thing the Constitution was. It was the Constitution of the people of the country, and under it, here today, before the American Senate, he felt that he was a man and an American citizen. . . . Turning toward Mr. Chase, Mr. Johnson said: 'And your exaltation and position depend upon the people.' Then turning toward the Cabinet, he said: 'And I will say to you, Mr. Secretary Seward, and to you, Mr. Secretary Stanton, and to you, Mr. Secretary —' (To a gentleman nearby, *sotto voce*, 'Who is Secretary of the Navy?' The person addressed replied in a whisper, 'Mr. Welles')—and to you, Mr. Secretary Welles, I would say, you derive your power from the people.' Mr. Johnson then remarked that the great element of vitality in this government was its nearness and proximity to the people. He wanted to say to all who heard him in the face of the American people, that all power was derived from the people. He would say in the hearing of the foreign ministers, for he was going to tell the truth here today, that he was a plebeian—he thanked God for it."

By this time, despite the chattering of the women in the gallery, Johnson's audience, which was expecting the brief, formal speech that was customary for the occasion, had caught on to the fact that something was very wrong. The speaker's florid face and peculiar manner of speaking caused the unruly crowd to fall silent. The silence emphasized the lack of meaning in what was being said. The loud, pompous voice went on to boast several times more about its plebeian origin; then it drifted off to Tennessee, where God was again thanked that it was still a state in the Union although "there had been an interregnum, a hiatus."

---

* On March 9 Johnson wrote to Richard Sutton, chief reporter of the Senate, saying: "I see from the *Congressional Globe* that the proceedings of Saturday, the 4 inst. have not as yet been published, and as I understand there has been some criticism . . . will you . . . preserve the original notes . . . and bring me an accurate copy of your report of what I said on that occasion." The speech, as published in the *Globe* on March 17, is obviously rewritten.

It was obvious to everyone now that the Vice President-elect was trying to show off his political vocabulary but could not put the high-sounding words together to make sense.

The members of the House were crowding in before anyone could stop the unhappy speaker. The Democrats were secretly delighted at what was happening, but the Republicans took it badly. Senator Zachariah Chandler of Michigan wrote later to his wife: "I was never so mortified in my life. Had I been able to find a small hole, I should have dropped through it out of sight."

Amid audible remarks of "What a shame!" and "Tell him to stop," Johnson was temporarily silenced. Hamlin then tried to administer the oath of office quickly. But Johnson was in no condition to be hurried. Hamlin had to read the oath by single sentences and sometimes prompt the befuddled man.

Hamlin then adjourned the old Senate, and the new Vice President called the new Senate to order. But Johnson's ordeal was not yet over. Eight newly elected senators were called upon to take their oath of office. Johnson held out a Bible to them, so they could touch it and bow their heads. Then he dismissed them without formally giving them the oath. Some of the bewildered senators began leaving the stand. J. W. Forney, the clerk of the Senate, had to take over and recall them so he could administer the official oath of office. Since the weather was rapidly improving, he then announced that the procession to the east front of the building should be formed.

The great occasion had begun badly, and there was much shaking of heads when the people who had been in the Senate chamber went outside to seek places on the platform. It was the first inauguration to be held in front of the new iron dome, which had been completed on December 2, 1863, when the head of Thomas Crawford's statue of Freedom was hauled into place.

The New York *Herald*'s correspondent tells how the platform quickly filled up: "Ladies, Senators, Negroes, Justices, secretaries, diplomats, and people generally, tumbled upon the platform pell-mell. As the ladies moved on to the north entrance there was a grand national display of ankles. Representative ankles were exhibited by the fair dames and lasses of every state in the Union. The variety of shape and size of hose was perfectly bewildering; but every foot was muddy and every skirt bedraggled. . . . Colored persons innumerable flocked around, though none were admitted to the Capitol. Soldiers off duty were present in large numbers. . . . Men, women and children soaked about quietly, caught cold, and waited . . . The rain had taken all the starch out of them.

CONTINUED ON PAGE 94

UNWANTED TREASURES

of the Patent Office

Thousands of products of Yankee genius, in miniature models, have

survived a British invasion, three fires, and a sale at Gimbels

By DONALD W. HOGAN

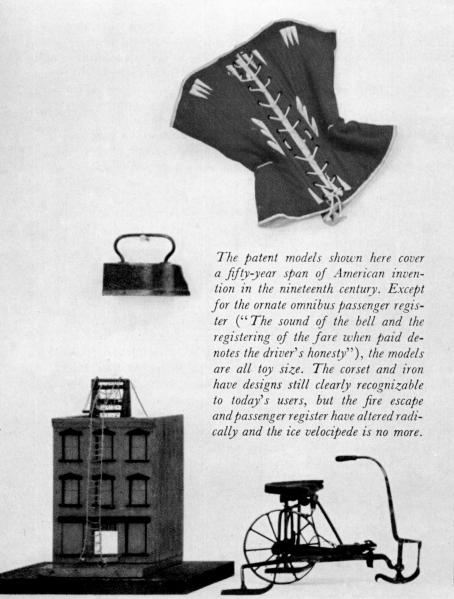

The patent models shown here cover a fifty-year span of American invention in the nineteenth century. Except for the ornate omnibus passenger register ("*The sound of the bell and the registering of the fare when paid denotes the driver's honesty*"), the models are all toy size. The corset and iron have designs still clearly recognizable to today's users, but the fire escape and passenger register have altered radically and the ice velocipede is no more.

While the British were busily engaged in putting the torch to Washington on the evening of August 24, 1814, Dr. William Thornton, superintendent of the Patent Office, stood aghast by a window in Georgetown watching the Capitol, of which he was the chief designer, go up in flames. But the next morning, when he learned that the Patent Office too was threatened with fire, he mounted a horse and dashed back into the city, one of the first Americans to return.

Quickly he approached a Colonel Jones, who had been assigned to burn that part of the city, and begged that Blodgett's Hotel, which a few years before had become the Patent Office and museum for its models, be spared from the flames. According to his own report, he stood amid the smoldering ruins of the city and successfully overwhelmed the Britisher by charging that the destruction of "the building . . . which contained . . . hundreds of models of the arts . . . would be as barbarous as formerly to burn the Alexandrian Library for which the Turks have since been condemned by all enlightened nations." Blodgett's Hotel was the

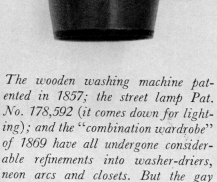

The wooden washing machine patented in 1857; the street lamp Pat. No. 178,592 (it comes down for lighting); and the "combination wardrobe" of 1869 have all undergone considerable refinements into washer-driers, neon arcs and closets. But the gay "Hot Atmosphere and Medicated Bath," with separate entrances for men and women, evidently did not catch on.

The model for a candle mold (above) is a rare one, as it was patented in 1836 before the numbering of the models began. The "blind slat adjuster," Pat. No. 15,758, is a forerunner of the modern venetian blind.

Patent Commissioner Thomas E. Robertson inspects a few samples from the mountain of models sold in 1925. The umbrella is recognizable, but not what was new about it. Is the gadget on the right a sewing machine? No one is sure.

only government building spared in the razing of Washington.

This seems to have been the high point of the federal government's concern for its collection of patent models, which since that time has been decimated by three other fires, two federal economy waves, three auctions, a bankruptcy, and a sale at Gimbels.

Seven weeks before the last of the thirteen original states ratified the Constitution, Secretary of State Thomas Jefferson, Secretary of War Henry Knox, and Attorney General Edmund Randolph became the Patent Commission. When they opened for business on April 10, 1790, they immediately established the requirement that a working model of each invention, done in miniature, be submitted as part of the application.

This requirement was kept in force until 1870, when a change in the law was made necessary by quarters so bulging with models that there was no room for examiners, and the submission of a model was made discretionary with the commissioner of patents. By 1880 the requirement was dropped altogether with the wry exception of flying machines—for which the requirement was also dropped after 1903 and Kitty Hawk.

(But the Patent Office still demands physical proof of the pudding before it will issue a patent for a perpetual motion machine.)

From the very start the models—the idea for which sounds like a Jeffersonian notion—became a tail that wagged the dog. Their number and bulk dictated the division's move in 1810 from an office in the Department of State to Blodgett's Hotel. Congress had appropriated $10,000 to purchase the hotel and $3,000 to renovate it, insisting that the two larger of four rooms assigned to the Patent Office be devoted to displaying the models. The rest of the building, except for two smaller rooms, was given over to the General Post Office.

Congress would brook no untidiness in the exhibition. A committee reported within three months of the appropriation that "although many models have already been deposited in their new quarters, the manner in which they are placed tends to confusion and to sink the establishment into contempt. It is hoped that habit will not operate to make this perpetual."

The chiding was effective, and Blodgett's Hotel, which had originally housed the United States Theater, the first in Washington, regained and even surpassed its earlier fame as a point of interest for travelers to the capital. Foreign visitors were shown the models as a proud demonstration of American inventiveness, and on Sundays it became a local custom to stroll through the rooms and see what was new.

But, even though the models were the focal point of interest in the Patent Office, no record of their kind or number appears to have been made until January 21, 1823, when, for no apparent reason, a clerk at least attempted a listing.

His catalogue showed a nation still more concerned with agriculture and building pursuits than with industrial development. It listed 95 nail cutters, 66 pumps, and 65 plows as against 45 looms, 28 spinning machines, and 3 boring machines. Of "propelling boats" there were 38; of carding machines, 8; of threshing machines, 20; and of winnowing machines, 25. There were 13 bridges, 26 sawmills, 17 water mills, 7 windmills, 14 steam mills, 26 water wheels, 56 presses, 3 stocking looms, 10 fire engines, 1 machine for making barrels, 6 flax-dressing machines, 6 file-cutting machines, 16 cloth-shearing machines, 10 straw cutters, 12 locks, and 2 guns. The specific listings came to 635 and evidently so exhausted the cataloguer that he lumped the remaining 1,184 models as for "various other purposes" and gave a total of 1,819 models in all.

This was the only listing of the models ever made—with the exception of one which was paid for in 1908 but which, when it was sorely needed in 1925, could not be found.

After 1823 the number of patent models at Blodgett's Hotel increased until by 1836 there were about 7,000 of them, lodged against more than 10,000 patents issued. A committee of Congress reporting on the need for a new building declared that "a great number of them, supposed to be 500, from want of room, have been stowed away in a dark garret." (It was an ominous precedent.) In July, 1836, a law was passed allowing for construction of the new building. Ground had hardly been broken, six months later, when at three o'clock on the morning of December 15 fire was discovered in the Post Office section of Blodgett's Hotel. Within a matter of hours the building was burned to the ground, and with it went every record and every model owned by the Patent Office.

Describing the calamity, a Senate investigating committee spoke ruefully of "a pride which must now stand rebuked by the improvidence which exposed so many memorials and evidences of the superiority of American genius to the destruction which has overtaken them." And Congress, perhaps impressed by this rhetoric, promptly appropriated $100,000 for restoration of "3,000 of the most important [models] . . . which will form a very interesting and valuable collection."

At first Patent Commissioner Henry L. Ellsworth worked diligently both at having the burned models restored or rebuilt and at outfitting the showrooms of the new Patent Office. Shortly, however, he complained to the secretary of state, under whose department his office came, that many inventors had failed to co-oper-

Dr. William Thornton, superintendent of patents who saved the models when the British burned Washington, was a painter, architect, and pioneer inventor who helped design a pre-Fulton steamboat and held eight other patents of his own.

ate and that it was impossible to remake the models without their help. This was particularly true of such inventions as the plow with cannon for handles to fight off sudden Indian attack—of which the burnt model was the only one ever made.

But if Ellsworth was thwarted by the apathy of inventors when it came to restoring models, he was overcome by their enthusiasm for submitting new ones. The new Patent Office building at Seventh to Ninth between F and G was only partially completed by 1844, but already the Commissioner was forced to complain that unless the job were hurried the collection of models would force the working staff out onto the street. "The increase of models renders daily the transaction of business more difficult," Ellsworth wrote in his annual report. (In fact, he was so discouraged by the influx of new models that he managed to spend only $25,588.91 of the $100,000 appropriated for restoration of the old ones.)

By 1856, however, three wings of the new building were completed. Its great halls, the east and west wings, were fitted out as showrooms, and the building again became a tourist attraction, a display of national ingenuity.

Then came the Civil War. Invention was fantastically stimulated. Models, which had been coming in by the hundreds every year, now arrived by the thousands. Several of them came each day to each of the twenty examiners and were thrown on shelves until papers were completed and issued. Then, just as quickly, the models were tagged with basic information and carted to the galleries, unclassified, where higgledy-piggledy they were tossed into a case or onto another shelf. An army shoe would land next to a drill; a corset beside a sword.

By 1876, William H. Doolittle, acting commissioner of patents, reported that the building was so clogged with models that the public had been barred from seeing them for lack of room.

He estimated that 175,000 models had been crowded into the galleries and that they were increasing by 13,000 to 14,000 a year. "Immediate relief," he said, "is necessary." Even though a law of 1870 had made the submission of models discretionary, it appeared the Commissioner had not wanted to take upon himself the responsibility for rejecting them. But neither could he function in their midst.

Temporary relief came on September 24, 1877, when fire again broke out in the Patent Office. Although the blaze was confined to the west and north wings, and neither of them was destroyed, 160 cases of models, estimated to contain 76,000 in all, were ruined.

Some of these were replaced through a $45,000 ap-

CONTINUED ON PAGE 101

PANDEMONIUM *at* PROMONTORY

The official painting is

full of dignity and decorum lamentably absent in the actual photograph

By LUCIUS BEEBE

Historians are agreed that the most dramatic and at the same time the most significant single date in the record of the American West was May 10, 1869, when the rails of the Union Pacific and the Central Pacific railroads met and were joined at Promontory Point, a desolate spot in the Utah desert, about forty miles northwest of Ogden. Here in a single day and hour worlds met head-on, the American people achieved a continental dimension, Manifest Destiny was realized, and the Old West reached its apotheosis. All that had gone before in the conquest of the American continent by white men was met and recapitulated in the driving of a spike of California gold in a ceremonial tie of laurel, along with a tie of Nevada silver from the Comstock Lode and another from Arizona of silver, gold, and iron in equal parts.

But Promontory's great hour was not only a shining moment of splendor and achievement of empire, it was also a scene of low comedy and lamentable moral tone that redeemed it forever from holy or virtuous significance. The details of Promontory's finest hour were just a little out of drawing.

To begin with, the Union Pacific train from the East was delayed by heavy rains and washouts in Weber Canyon and was a day late. The ceremonies were postponed from May 9, but no word of the change in plans reached San Francisco in time, with the result that the entire city closed up shop a day before the event it was celebrating and stayed at a fine pitch of patriotic alcoholism for three whole days.

The weather at Promontory was inclement. Low clouds and rain and a chill wind off Great Salt Lake made for discomfort. Collis Huntington, one of the Central's "Big Four," was in New York, while Charlie Crocker and Mark Hopkins, other members, had been

unable to leave Sacramento and San Francisco, respectively. Brigham Young, president of the Latter-day Saints, sent his excuses and stayed away in a huff because the right of way had avoided the Mormon capital at Salt Lake City. William Henry Jackson, greatest of western photographers, got mixed up in his dates and arrived a week after the excitement was over, but his place was taken by Colonel Charles Savage, who immortalized the event on wet plates in his enormous view camera, capturing the scene at a moment when a timid sun emerged briefly from behind the dull gray clouds.

But if a number of distinguished guests who should have been present were elsewhere than at Promontory Point, a considerable number of celebrants arrived to maintain to the end the low and joyous moral tone which had characterized the progress of the Union Pacific all the way from Omaha and constituted the "Hell on Wheels" that accompanied the track-laying gangs across Nebraska, Colorado, Wyoming, and part of Utah. A generous contingent of prostitutes arrived from Corrine, a construction camp a few miles down the track. "They contributed a quota of furbelows," recorded Edwin Sabin, the U.P.'s official historian, delicately, but their presence was the occasion of hard looks from the Reverend John Todd of Pittsfield, Massachusetts, imported to lend piety to the doings.

Then, too, the construction workers themselves displayed a lamentable lack of restraint. Bottles passed freely from hand to hand amidst uncouth salutations, to show up prominently in Colonel Savage's official photograph of the great moment.

At the ceremony itself contretemps of a minor nature gathered and multiplied. Everyone had to wait on the Western Union telegrapher, who was testing the circuits that would instantly convey to Washington,

THE UNGLAMOROUS TRUTH *of Promontory is recorded in Savage's wet-plate photograph. As the Central Pacific's Jupiter (left) meets No. 119 of the Union Pacific, the two chief engineers, S. S. Montague (left) and Grenville M. Dodge, shake hands. They are the only notables in evidence. The champagne bottles being brandished above their heads have been whited out in earlier publications of this photograph and do not appear at all in the dignified painting on the next two pages.*

New York, Boston, Philadelphia, and other great eastern cities the news that the spike had been driven. When the gold spike itself was inserted in the hole prepared for it, President Leland Stanford of the Central Pacific took a mighty swipe at it with the official silver spike maul and missed by a generous margin. There was rude laughter among the numerous experts present. Vice President Thomas C. Durant likewise missed. A professional, General Jack Casement, head of U.P. construction, finally smote the spike home amidst ironical cheers from the Paddies.

When Colonel Savage's historic wet plate was developed, the result was beyond all question the most important single photograph in the iconography of the Old West, but it wasn't altogether satisfactory to Stanford. It was raffish in its general tone, uncouth, and, for a perpetual candidate for public honors, a bit boozy. Three champagne bottles showed in the precise center of the picture, and the presence of others was strongly suggested. Stanford himself didn't show up in the group and neither did the imported man of God.

From Stanford's viewpoint it was all most unfortunate.

Stanford, therefore, commissioned Thomas Hill, an understanding portrait painter, to clean up history a little, and Hill set about including the likenesses of seventy citizens of blameless life in one of the greatest portrait studies in the history of art. It was also one of the most monumental historic fakes. No ladies from Corrine appeared in the finished masterpiece. There were no bottles. A look of appropriate solemnity was on every bearded face. Included were at least four persons who hadn't actually been present—Stanford's three associates, Crocker, Hopkins, and Huntington, and Theodore Judah, original engineer of the Central Pacific, who had been dead for years. Conspicuous in the foreground were the Reverend John Todd and, of course, the well-composed features of Leland Stanford.

Even though Hill's painting had been tailored to his explicit directions, Stanford, when he saw the finished work, wanted no part of it, any more than he had of Colonel Savage's photograph. Several people

21

whom he felt might be useful to him politically did not appear very prominently.

The painting hangs today in the California capitol in Sacramento, a bogus re-creation of a dramatic and hilarious moment in American history, an object for mirth, pity, or cynicism, whichever may move the individual beholder.

Lucius Beebe, a regular contributor to AMERICAN HERITAGE, *is the publisher of the Virginia City, Nevada,* Territorial Enterprise, *once edited by Mark Twain. He is the author of many books on railroading, including (with Charles Clegg) the recent* Age of Steam.

THE GLAMOROUS FICTION *is preserved in Thomas Hill's painting, done at Leland Stanford's direction. At center Stanford (6), president of the Central Pacific, prepares to drive the golden spike held by F. L. Vandenberg (5), head of the Central Pacific telegraph department. The Reverend Dr. John Todd (3) offers the invocation. Behind him stand E. H. Miller, Jr., secretary of the Central Pacific (1) and James W. Haynes of the United States Railroad Commission (2). The three men who, with Stanford formed the Central's "Big Four" were not actually present, but Hill painted them in anyway. They are Collis P. Huntington (7), a vice president; Mark Hopkins (11), treasurer; and Charles Crocker (14), who*

STATE OF CALIFORNIA DEPARTMENT OF FINANCE; COURTESY *Li*

supervised the building of the Central Pacific line. Nor was Theodore Judah (15), the Central Pacific's founder, present; he had died in 1863. Union Pacific officials include Thomas C. Durant (4), a vice president; Oakes Ames (8), substituting for his brother Oliver, also a vice president; Sidney Dillon (9), chairman of the board; and General Grenville M. Dodge (10), the famous railroad engineer who had directed the laying of the Union Pacific tracks. S. S. Montague (16) and S. W. Sanderson (17) were chief engineer and counselor, respectively, for the Central Pacific. The two ladies with a trackside view of the spike-driving are Miss Earl (12), otherwise unidentified, and Mrs. S. B. Reed (13), wife of a Union Pacific official.

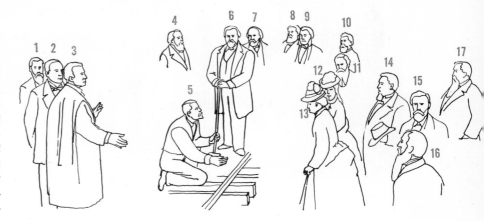

23

FUNSTON *Captures* AGUINALDO

UNCLE SAM---COME INSIDE, YOU YOUNG RASCAL; I'M TIRED OF CHASING YOU AROUND IN THE WET.

m almost met his match

By WILLIAM F. ZORNOW

Emilio Aguinaldo poses in his general's uniform shortly after the revolt began. At 29 he was already an experienced guerrilla leader. His captor, General Frederick Funston (above, left), appears in a photograph taken several years afterward.

In the relatively uneventful spring of 1901, news of an army officer's daring exploit in a newly acquired possession across the Pacific was the talk of America. By an elaborate ruse General Frederick Funston had captured Emilio Aguinaldo, guiding spirit of the insurrection in the Philippine Islands. Since the Filipinos had no other leader of Aguinaldo's prowess, it was apparent that the small but exasperating war, which for two years had engaged an American expeditionary force of 70,000, was virtually over.

Today few remember the names of Funston or Aguinaldo; for that matter, the Philippine Insurrection and America's brief flirtation with imperialism at the turn of the century are all but forgotten. Yet the era is not without significance, because these were the years when, for the first time in its history, the United States extended its territorial jurisdiction beyond the limits of continental North America—and in the process became a world power.

Very soon after the brief war with Spain ended in the summer of 1898, the United States suddenly found itself with its first colonial problem. The Filipinos had expected independence, and when instead the islands were annexed by the United States, many of their "liberated" people, far from welcoming American rule, soon came to dislike the new masters as much as the old ones. Unlike some Americans, they did not view annexation as an act of humanity toward an ignorant, downtrodden, and backward people; and on February 4, 1899, two days before the Senate ratified the annexation treaty, Filipino insurgents attacked the American expeditionary force stationed in and around Manila.

At first it seemed an easy matter to put down the insurrection, for in fight after fight the Americans beat back the disorganized and poorly equipped rebel army. Finally realizing that they could not win by conventional means of warfare, thousands of Filipinos resorted to guerrilla tactics, and the struggle became a grim series of sudden ambuscades, brutal reprisals, and small patrol actions in the jungle—a type of combat for which the harassed Americans were totally unprepared. Once the rebels discarded their uniforms, the transformation from soldier to civilian was simply a matter of hiding rifle and bolo in the brush. Villagers who turned out of their thatched huts to wave flags and shout *"amigo"* at passing American columns became *insurrectos* again the moment the troops faded from sight.

This plan of resistance did have an Achilles' heel, however, for it was predicated on the guiding spirit of one man, Aguinaldo, who led the insurgent army and who had proclaimed himself president of the Philippine Republic. A wiry, boyish-looking little man who weighed only 115 pounds, Aguinaldo was a veteran of revolutionary activity in the cause of Philippine independence. To the superstitious natives—and to the Americans as well—he seemed to possess *"anting-anting,"* a mystical power to resist bullets and capture.

After nearly two years of frustrating warfare against the guerrillas, American military authorities concluded that the revolt would never be broken until Aguinaldo was killed or captured. The trouble was that intelligence officers had been totally unable to discover his whereabouts and knew only that rebel army commanders received orders from a clandestine headquarters somewhere on Luzon Island. It was a mystery which remained unsolved until a chance occurrence revealed Aguinaldo's hiding place to Funston, a tough little army officer from Kansas.

Funston had spent a large part of his 36 years wandering—a soldier of fortune in a real sense. Five feet five inches tall, he had the stocky, well-muscled build of a bantamweight boxer. A competent botanist (although he never finished college), he served for several years as a special agent of the Department of Agriculture, a job which took him on expeditions to such places as Death Valley and Alaska—where he once made a 1,500-mile canoe trip down the Yukon River.

Passing through New York City early in 1896, Funston volunteered to join the Cuban insurgents in their revolution against Spain. Always hungry for excitement, he enlisted as an artillery officer even though he had never fired a field piece. A few weeks in an attic with a small cannon and an instruction manual gave him enough knowledge to qualify, and in August 1896 he was smuggled into Cuba. There he fought for eighteen months, returning home just before the outbreak of the Spanish-American War. On the basis of his Cuban experience, he was made commander of the 20th Kansas Regiment, which sailed for the Philippine Islands in the fall of 1898.

Although Funston arrived too late to fight the Spanish—who had surrendered a few months after Dewey's victory in May—he saw plenty of action in the insurrection. Leading his troops in 38 engagements, he was wounded once and rose in rank from colonel to brigadier general of volunteers. At the battle of Calumpit, he particularly distinguished himself. Under heavy fire he crossed a 400-foot river on a raft and with a small group of men established a bridgehead, which he held until reinforcements arrived to solidify the position. For his performance in this action he was awarded the Congressional Medal of Honor.

On February 8, 1901, Funston was at his headquarters at San Isidro on Luzon Island when a detachment of American troops reported the surrender of some rebels in a nearby village. To be sure, rebels drifted into the American lines daily, offering to take the oath of allegiance; but this particular party happened to be commanded by Cecilio Segismundo, Aguinaldo's trusted messenger. Furthermore, Segismundo was reported to be carrying some important dispatches.

Suspecting that this might be a significant development, Funston ordered Segismundo and the dispatches rushed to San Isidro. Under questioning the Filipino admitted that he was connected with Aguinaldo and identified the village of Palanan, in the mountainous northern reaches of Luzon, as the rebel headquarters. Segismundo told Funston that there were no more than fifty guards at Palanan, adding that even the villagers were unaware that the famous leader was in their midst. Aguinaldo was known to them simply as "Captain Emilio."

Delaying judgment as to whether or not Segismundo was telling the truth, Funston then turned to the dispatches, many of which were in code. A closer examination revealed that some were signed with the names "Pastor" and "Colon Magdalo," which were pseudonyms often used by Aguinaldo. The handwriting of the signatures was unmistakably his, so there could be no doubt that the dispatches were genuine.

Funston, another American officer, and Lazaro Segovia, a trusted intelligence agent who understood English, Spanish, and the Tagalog dialect of the islands, labored all night over the code. By morning, the messages were deciphered. Unfortunately they did not mention the location of Aguinaldo's headquarters but indicated that this information was known by the bearer. Funston concluded that Segismundo had been telling the truth.

One of Funston's first plans was to land a military force close to Palanan from a gunboat and march overland to the capital; but Segismundo warned that such an operation would be instantly detected. Actually an American column had entered Palanan some months before but had found nothing. Segismundo's explanation was that the approach of the Americans had been reported and that the dictator had fled to the hills with his staff and archives.

Some other method would have to be found. At length, Funston concluded that Aguinaldo's dispatches provided him with the method whereby the capture could be effected. The most important message was an order to Baldomero Aguinaldo, the dictator's cousin, instructing him to assume command of all guerrilla operations in central Luzon. He was further ordered to have his subordinate commanders send some companies of crack troops to headquarters for Aguinaldo's personal service.

Funston decided to disguise some loyal Filipinos and send them to Palanan posing as the men Aguinaldo had requested. Funston and a few other American officers, disguised as prisoners of war, would accompany the column. The plan was submitted to American Headquarters, where it was approved by General Arthur MacArthur (father of General Douglas MacArthur). Later, when the expedition was ready to depart, MacArthur voiced his misgivings as he seized the brigadier's hand and said, "Funston, this is a desperate undertaking. I fear that I shall never see you again."

The plan was prepared with care. Funston handpicked 81 Macabebes, whose loyalty to the United States was intensified by their traditional hatred of Aguinaldo's Tagalogs. These Little Macs, as Funston dubbed his charges, were chosen because they spoke Tagalog in addition to their own dialect. They were armed with captured rebel rifles, and most of them were dressed as peasants, since few insurgents wore uniforms.

Since Funston was supposed to be a prisoner, the column would have to be under the command of Filipino officers. In addition to Segismundo, Funston picked Hilario Tal Placido, Lazaro Segovia, Dionisio Bató, and Gregorio Cadhit. Placido had been an officer in the rebel army before taking the oath of allegiance to the United States, and he knew Aguinaldo personally. To join him in acting as American prisoners (all the Americans were to be disguised as privates), Funston chose Captains Harry W. Newton and R. T. Hazzard, and Lieutenants Burton J. Mitchell and O. P. M. Hazzard. Newton knew something about the country through which the expedition would pass.

After sundown on March 6, 1901, the gunboat *Vicksburg* steamed out of Manila Bay with the expedition aboard. Once at sea, Funston revealed the nature of the adventure to his men. The ex-insurgent officers were visibly perturbed at being asked to go into the lion's den, but the Macabebes were enthusiastic about the project. Pedro Bustos, a sergeant who wore decorations conferred by the Spanish, spoke up proudly, "My General, I cannot speak for the others; but for myself, I am a soldier of the United States." Funston would have no difficulty with his Little Macs.

Although the plan had involved several weeks of preparation, it was actually quite simple. Segismundo had warned that no steamer could touch shore within 100 miles of rebel headquarters without being reported immediately by Aguinaldo's agents. So it was decided to leave the *Vicksburg* some miles at sea and paddle ashore in three *barcas*. These canoe-like sailboats were procured en route, but the seas ran heavily and they all swamped. So Funston was forced to run the risk of detection by having the *Vicksburg* approach the beach at night. The men then went ashore, and the steamer was again out of sight by dawn. Fortunately this operation was accomplished without incident or discovery. The expedition found itself ashore near its first objective, the village of Casiguran.

The next morning, March 14, the party set off for Casiguran. It was only a few miles away, but the sea was rough and it rained incessantly during the trip. The men followed the beach all the way, but mangrove thickets often came down to the water's edge, and the troops were forced to wade around them. As a result of the delay, the journey consumed the better part of one whole day, and when the men reached Casiguran they were completely exhausted and famished, since they had brought only enough food for breakfast. Although it was not much of a town, Casiguran proved a welcome sight. Funston, his fellow "prisoners," and the Macabebes had three days in which to recuperate before they resumed the journey.

While resting at Casiguran, Funston put the plan into operation. He had prepared letters for Aguinaldo, and these were sent to rebel headquarters from Casiguran. One letter, purportedly from Placido, recounted

how his column, while en route to rebel headquarters with Segismundo, had encountered a small force of Americans, with whom a skirmish had been fought. Five of the Americans had been captured and were being brought to headquarters for questioning. In this manner Funston prepared Aguinaldo to accept the presence of some Americans so close to his hiding place.

Under ordinary circumstances Aguinaldo might have been suspicious of this message, but Funston had added a master touch to give it an authenticity above question. Another letter allegedly came from Lacuna, one of Aguinaldo's commanders in Luzon. In this letter, Funston, in the role of Lacuna, said that in accordance with instructions from Baldomero Aguinaldo he was sending eighty men to the rebel capital under command of Placido, Segovia, and Segismundo. This was in keeping with instructions contained in the messages Segovia had decoded at San Isidro.

During the previous October, Funston had had a brush with Lacuna in which he had captured the rebel's personal property, including some stationery with the words "Brigada Lacuna" printed at the top of each sheet. An expert forger in Manila had imitated Lacuna's signature on some of them, and it was on these that Funston wrote his message to Aguinaldo. The signature and letterhead deceived Aguinaldo completely, and he accepted the message as being genuine.

The Macabebes had a holiday at Casiguran as the village band turned out to do them homage, and the

THE NATIONAL ARCHIVES

U.S. soldiers, armed with the hard-kicking Springfield rifles nicknamed "smoke wagons," dig in against Aguinaldo's men. The G.I. in the foreground seems to have scant respect for the marksmanship of the Filipinos.

27

inhabitants clustered around to hear of their gallant victory over Funston's men. The Little Macs proved to be consummate liars and took much delight in expanding their stories. Funston was justifiably worried that they might overdo it and arouse suspicion, forget themselves and speak in their native dialect rather than Tagalog, or fail to treat the Americans as prisoners. A deference for officers was something the Spanish had instilled in them, and it was extremely difficult for Funston to convince his Macs that they would have to treat him and the other American officers as prisoners of war.

Worrisome as these problems were, they were the least of Funston's headaches. In Casiguran he heard that Aguinaldo had been reinforced by 400 men. Five to one odds were sufficient cause for alarm, but Funston assured his men that the element of surprise would more than compensate for this disparity in force.

The principal danger, however, was a lack of provisions. It was a seven-day march to Palanan and the *alcalde*, or mayor, of Casiguran could supply enough food for only three days. The terrain was known to be the roughest and most difficult in Luzon. The *alcalde* offered to have enough food available in a week, but Funston did not dare delay that long because the *Vicksburg* was scheduled to arrive at Palanan Bay on March 25. If Funston did not bag his quarry and arrive before that date, the gunboat's appearance would send Aguinaldo packing into the hills. Further delay at Casiguran was unthinkable.

The expedition set out for its final destination, trusting to luck that the provisions on hand would be sufficient. There were other dangers and mishaps. Funston took along twelve men from Casiguran to act as bearers, and he was still concerned that his Macabebes might betray the plan to them by speaking in their own dialect. This did not happen, but before the first day's hike ended, the enterprise was jeopardized by the desertion of the party's guide. Fortunately one of the Casiguran bearers thought he knew the way to Palanan, and the expedition pressed forward.

The rain continued to fall daily. Although the column hugged the beach, it was still necessary to bypass mangrove thickets by wading in the heavy surf, to ford innumerable streams, and to ascend precipitous cliffs which rose directly from the water's edge. Even where the beach was wide enough to permit passage, progress was delayed by innumerable boulders ranging in size from watermelons to boxcars.

The meager three-day rations were stretched to last five days by partaking of only two meals daily, supplementing them with a "revolting mess" of stewed snails,

limpets, and devilfish. On the fifth night the men lay down supperless. The column was rapidly approaching the limit of endurance as the exhausted men reeled along the trail without any semblance of order. Uppermost in Funston's tired brain was the thought that 450 men at Aguinaldo's camp still had to be fought; the Macabebes, in their weakened condition, were no match for a dozen.

Ironically, it was Funston's good fortune to be rescued by Aguinaldo himself. The dictator had received the forged letters and dispatched a man to intercept the approaching column. This envoy arrived on the sixth night and presented to the Filipino officers a message from Simon Villa, Aguinaldo's chief of staff. Provisions could be sent from Palanan. There was one dark spot, however, for Villa ordered that the American prisoners were to be left at Dinundungan. It would be impolitic, he said, to bring them to Palanan, where they would discover the dictator's presence.

This is a somewhat inaccurate version of Funston's exploit at the battle of Calumpit, April 26, 1899. Actually two privates, both undressed, swam the river under fire, moored a rope, and pulled across a raft carrying Funston and his men. Funston won the Medal of Honor for holding this beachhead until reinforcements arrived. Here, however, he is first on the rope; he is also seen in the oval at upper right.

on the unpredictability of army ways, sent the prisoners along with the ten Macabebes who had been left as guards.

Palanan and success were only eight miles away, but within sight of the goal Funston began to falter. His splendid physique, perfected by years of campaigning and exploring, now began to collapse. He moved forward under great strain and every hundred yards was forced to lie prostrate for a few minutes to regain his breath. The rear guard moved at a snail's pace.

Suddenly there emerged from the bushes ahead of them a panting Macabebe sergeant, running at top speed, who waved them into a thicket and held up his other hand for silence. Funston and the others had scarcely reached the protection of some bamboo and brush when the reason for the warning became apparent. A small band of rebels was coming toward them along the trail. The gaily chatting *insurrectos* passed within a few feet of the crouching Americans.

As it turned out, these were a group of rebel officers from Palanan en route to guard the prisoners. At the head of the main column, Placido and Segovia had moved ahead with all possible speed after sending the faked letter to Dinundungan. When they met the rebel guards, Segovia had engaged them in conversation for a moment, while signaling to the sergeant to scurry back and warn Funston.

About the time Funston and his men were crouching in the undergrowth, the main party had reached the Palanan River, which proved to be about 100 yards wide, swollen from the rain. On the opposite bank stood Aguinaldo's hideout. Segovia and Placido crossed the stream in a *barca* and made their way toward Aguinaldo, who stood before his headquarters with seven of his officers. Since the one available *barca* held only eight men, it would take at least half an hour to ferry the rest of the command across.

Aguinaldo took the two officers to his residence. While Placido answered questions and gave a verbose, time-consuming description of their magnificent victory over the American patrol and their capture of five of its members, Segovia stood near the window and watched the ferrying operation, well aware that any slip might betray the plot before the Macabebes had crossed.

It was a torturous thirty minutes, but Placido played

The town of Dinundungan actually proved to exist in name only. When the expedition arrived there, it found an old man supervising a few natives, who were building huts for the prisoners. Food arrived from Palanan, and the Macabebes and the prisoners revived their spirits with a hearty meal; but even more revivifying was the news that Aguinaldo had not received the 400 reinforcements. He had only the fifty guards that Segismundo had previously mentioned.

During the night Funston, Placido, and Segovia held a conference, and again the General utilized his facile pen. It was arranged that the Macs would leave the next morning and that an hour after the departure a false message would be sent back to the jailer instructing him to send the prisoners forward. This was done to allay the old man's suspicions. The next day everything went according to plan. The decoy message arrived, and the jailer, after a few comments

CONTINUED ON PAGE 107

29

George Armstrong Custer

Patrick Henry O'Rorke

George A. Woodruff

Adelbert Ames

Classmates

On the eve of the Civil W

north, others south, but their acade

It was just a century last summer since a tall, raw-boned Ohio farm boy stepped from the two o'clock boat to West Point's South Dock. He shouldered his baggage and climbed the steep path to the plain. Sun-drenched fields, dipping elms, indigo hills, and silver river spread out before him: the almost unbelievable beauty which would be the backdrop of his life for the next four years.

He stood for a few moments, awkward and shy, more alone than he had ever felt in all his seventeen years; more alone than he would ever feel again until his years had reached thirty-seven. Then he made the necessary inquiries, reported to the necessary places, signed the necessary papers in a bold, splashing hand, and became that lowest form of animal life—a new cadet.

His family and close friends had always called him Autie. His classmates took one good look at his rather long, Hessian-yellow hair and joyously dubbed him "Fanny." In the footnotes of the history books and in innumerable Western films he comes down to us as General George Armstrong Custer.

He is just about the only member of his class who *does* come down to us!

Yet there were others, once well-known, all still deserving of remembrance; and they were a fated group, for a pathetic conflict of loyalties and emotions was their lot when they left the Military Academy. In all the long history of West Point no cadets had gone forth into a more tragic world than the ones who left in the spring of 1861.

There is a strange and romantic haze resting on the high plain that overlooks the Hudson at West Point —that plain where so many of America's greatest soldiers, living briefly in a world apart, learned the rudiments of their demanding profession. But there is an especially somber and haunting hue to the atmosphere of the late 1850's, for the country was breaking apart,

Divided

ffering loyalties sent some West Pointers

iendships survived the conflict

By MARY ELIZABETH SERGENT

John Pelham

Joseph Wheeler

Fitzhugh Lee

Thomas Lafayette Rosser

S. Dodson Ramseur

and the line of fracture ran straight across the special world inhabited by young West Pointers.

Many things are learned at West Point; among them, the great fact of comradeship, the bond that ties together men dedicated to a common calling. And in the spring of 1861 the southern states were seceding from the Union, and war was upon the land, and so in a very short time many of the former West Point comrades were in opposition armies, fighting against one another. Some of them lived and some of them died, but all of them knew the strange, sad mixture of enmity and personal affection that was the peculiar heritage of the classes of 1861.

The word "classes" is used advisedly, for West Point sent forth two groups in that tragic spring of fire and conflict. The War Department had briefly tried the experiment of a five-year course in place of the normal four years; so the men who had become cadets in 1856 were due to graduate in the month of May, 1861, just ahead of the men who had entered in 1857 and would get their diplomas in June. Of the latter group, twenty-three men left when their states seceded, and thirty-four were graduated—of whom four immediately resigned to "go south." Of the five-year men, five resigned when their states left the Union, and eight more resigned immediately after their graduation in May. (More correctly, they tried to resign; the war was on by then, and the War Department ordered these men dismissed for "tendering resignation in the face of the enemy.") In any case, thirty-seven of the May graduates went to Washington, were commissioned in the U.S. Army, and set to work turning new recruits into soldiers.

All in all, of these two 1861 classes forty-five young officers fought, on one side or the other, at the first Battle of Bull Run, which came in mid-July. One of the most distinguished of the May group, Adelbert Ames, was almost killed there.

31

In May Mr. Ames had been a cadet captain. In July he was a very green lieutenant of the old 5th Artillery, a Regular Army outfit. He was a serious young man with grave dark eyes and a straight nose in a round face. He had graduated fifth in his class, and he was anxious to do the right thing in his first battle.

Although wounded, Ames refused to leave the field. The gunners propped him up on a caisson, obeyed his whispered orders diligently, and told themselves this lad, at least, had the makings of a good officer. Eventually he fainted, fell off the caisson, and was carried back to a hospital. He did not leave until September.

He survived; men from Rockland, Maine, are hard to kill. In fact Adelbert Ames reached the age of 97—the last survivor of his class. And in 1893 the government got around to giving him the Medal of Honor for his conduct on 21 July 1861. He was one of five from the May class to receive this award; the others were Eugene Beaumont, Samuel Benjamin, Henry Dupont, and Guy Henry.

Other soldiers got other awards, including that odd sort of promotion, in style then, known as brevet rank. This was, so to speak, a sort of unofficial promotion—a major might be given a brevet as a colonel, which meant that for the time being, and under certain circumstances, he could actually be a colonel, although his permanent rank was still that of major. One of the good things about the award of a brevet promotion was that the next of kin of a man who died while holding brevet rank was supposed to receive a higher pension, based on the brevet rather than the permanent rank.

Thus little Edmund Kirby, dying of his wounds three weeks after the Battle of Chancellorsville in 1863, was much cheered by a visit from the President of the United States. Mr. Lincoln made the young first lieutenant a brigadier general of volunteers on the spot. Kirby was 23, the son of an army paymaster's widow, and the sole support of his mother and sisters.

He had been wounded while helping rescue some guns for a volunteer battery. The contract surgeon who dressed his wound bungled the job; after Kirby was sent to a hospital in Washington, infection set in and the leg was amputated. But it was too late—medical science of the day could not do much once an infection took hold—and Kirby was told that he could not recover.

At West Point he had been a leader in cadet prayer meetings. He was not afraid, but he grieved for the mother and sisters he must leave behind. Now, as the tall shadow of Abraham Lincoln receded on the hospital wall, he turned his cheek gratefully on the pillow and gave up his young life with a smile. The new rank assured an adequate pension.

His classmates in both armies grieved when they heard of his death. They grieved for many friends in those hard years. Looking back, one is surprised at a feeling which still comes down from those classes through all the smoke of battle. For that feeling is love! They were very hard fighters, yet those young men from West Point quite literally loved their enemies. That was one great thing West Point had given them, and it stayed with them through years of deadly combat.

It came to them naturally, out of the very air they had breathed as cadets, and its survival through the war is one of the haunting things that makes it worthwhile to take a glance now, a century afterward, at the Military Academy as it was in the years just before 1861.

In those days West Point was a very small, isolated village, almost wholly cut off from the outside world during the long winter months, remote enough at the best of times. The cadet corps was very small. There were only four companies—A, B, C, and D—each having fewer than seventy members. The cadets began their lives together at an impressionable age. The average new cadet in the 1850's was seventeen and a half years old when he entered the academy—the oldest just twenty-one, the youngest an unshaven sixteen. Once members of the corps, these boys led an almost monastic life, compared to which today's Spartan regime seems positively relaxed.

In the four years (five years for the classes of 1859, 1860, and May, 1861) they had one furlough. It began near the middle of June, two years after their arrival; it ended when the 2 P.M. boat touched the South Dock on August 28. There were no trips to athletic contests, no week ends, no breaks in the routine of their days. Unless granted leave by the secretary of war because of death or serious illness at home, they did not leave the post. A weekly exception was made for the handful of Roman Catholic cadets. Since there was no chapel of their faith on the post, these boys attended Mass each Sunday in Highland Falls. The priest knew how many gray uniforms should appear in his congregation, too, and anyone cutting church received four demerits.

The only organized recreations were dancing, riding, and fencing—all more in the nature of necessities than sports. (Every officer had to be able to ride a horse and use a sword, and on the isolated western posts regular "hops" were one way of passing the long winters.) On Christmas night the fencing academy was lighted until tattoo, and the cadets performed waltz, polka, and quadrille to the music of the Military Academy Band. For the most part they danced with each other. Only during the too-brief summer months did young ladies manage to reach the post. Then there were dances, picnics, and the usual aimless strolling along the river paths.

Cadets, as always, had very little spare time and used it according to individual inclination. In the summer they swam; in the winter they skated. They hiked and rode, unencumbered by companions in hoop skirts. Some did a little sketching from the ruins of old Fort Putnam. Now and then these sketches grew into small oil paintings which were proudly mailed home. The cadets also, one must suspect, did quite a bit of resting in the warm grass around the old fort.

They wrote and very much enjoyed receiving letters. On Saturdays they read in the library. Magazines, the novels of Scott and Cooper, and a book entitled *Horse Shoe Robinson* were very popular. Not all the reading was fiction. Emory Upton (an excellent student and officer, he also wrote extensively on tactics and military history), as might be expected, gave himself two educations at once. His roommate, John Rodgers, matched him almost volume for volume. Alonzo Cushing, with a brother at Annapolis, dipped into naval history. Many plowed doggedly through biography, history, travel, and tactics. Cadets even read books which today, if read at all, are read only by girls.

Not all amusements were innocent. One mile down the river stood the cottage of Benny Havens, a former civilian employee who had been forever banished from West Point by Sylvanus Thayer himself. The food in the mess hall, prepared by contract caterers in those days, was terrible. The buckwheat cakes and roast turkey prepared by Benny's Dutch wife were delicious. It was for no good, however, that the cottage was best known. Benny Havens made the best hot rum flip in the Hudson Valley. On dark nights, when the skating was good, the authorities had an unnerving habit of raiding his place, which was strictly off limits to all cadets.

One of Havens' best customers, in the old days, had

West Point as the classes of 1861 knew it appears in this Currier & Ives lithograph. Four instructors confer between mortars taken in the Mexican War. Below is the peaceful Hudson.

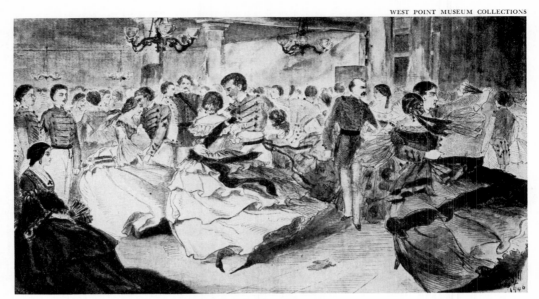

Cadets who generally danced with each other enjoyed a real "hop" like this one sketched by Winslow Homer in 1859. Hop managers (in sashes) that year included Cadets Ramseur, Ames, and Hazlett.

been Jefferson Davis—who later, as secretary of war, was the final authority over the Military Academy and all its works, and who, still later, was to be president of the Confederacy. Indeed, Davis was almost killed one night when he fell down a cliff while making a successful escape from Benny Havens' place during a raid. One wonders if he remembered that escapade when the case of Cadet Justin Dimick came before him. Mr. Dimick had been absent and off limits without leave. It was his second offense. The Secretary was graciously pleased to give him another chance upon the boy's pledge never again to violate paragraphs 115 and 116 of the Regulations. Four years later Justin Dimick gave his life for the Union at Chancellorsville.

The cadets worked hard, played hard, and occasionally fought hard; differences of opinion were settled with fists in the cold morning dew beneath the ramparts of old Fort Clinton. Hazing was in vogue, but most of it seems to have taken the form of rather innocent practical jokes. The cadets were almost completely dependent on their classmates for companionship, and the friendships they formed were expected to last a lifetime of dreary, lonely, and dangerous frontier duty. In actual fact those friendships did more than that; they even survived the trials of civil war, the hardest possible test for any friendship.

Time after time the old records tell the story. John Lea, Confederate States Army, had resigned from the June class when Mississippi left the Union. He was severely wounded and taken prisoner in the retreat from Williamsburg. As he recovered, he fell in love

with the daughter of the family which had nursed him. Finally they were married. Who stood up with the groom? George Armstrong Custer, United States Army.

"I am not disloyal when I tell you we heard with secret pride of his gallant deeds on the field of battle," wrote Adelbert Ames of Alabama's John Pelham. "It was what we had the right to expect of him—he was our classmate for five years—he was one of the best of us—who should win honors and glory if not he? And we were deeply grieved when we heard of his death."

These friendships extended beyond immediate class limits to bind all those who had been cadets together. "Late one night, while I was on my way from Montgomery to Atlanta just after the war," wrote Morris Schaff, class of 1862, "the ramshackle train stopped at a lonely station. Charles Ball [class of June, 1861], still in Confederate gray, entered. As soon as he recognized me, he quickened his step and met me with such unaffected cordiality that the car seemed to glow with new lamps. In view of what had gone before I would not have been hurt had he merely bowed and passed on, for I realized how much there had been to embitter. Yet he sat, and we talked over old times half the night. I could not help wondering, as he parted from me, whether I could have shown so much magnanimity had the South conquered the North, and had I come home in rags, to find the old farm desolate. I doubt it."

The impersonal records tell how the Confederate General Dodson Ramseur's headquarters flag was carried to the War Department in 1864—part of the booty Sheridan's men took when they defeated and captured that gallant graduate of 1860. But personal letters tell how the wounded Ramseur was carried to Sheridan's headquarters; how Union surgeons labored with a Southern doctor to save him; how friends in blue uniforms took down messages for Mrs. Ramseur and cut off a lock of brown hair for the baby daughter the young general would never see; and how, after long hours of agony, Dodson Ramseur died in the arms of his classmates.

One of the most enduring of these friendships was that between Custer and Thomas Lafayette Rosser. Rosser, three years older than Custer, was a member of the May class. He had been born in Virginia but was raised on a pioneer's farm in Texas. He was big—six feet, two inches—and strong in everything but book learning. Rosser roomed with John Pelham, and the three had one thing in common from the beginning: they were the best riders in the corps. If Custer, Pelham, or Rosser could not stay on a horse, that horse could not be ridden.

John Pelham was as fair as Rosser was dark. He was a quiet boy, a shade higher than the other two scholastically. He was one of the best-liked men in his class, and later in the Army of Northern Virginia. And he has probably had more children named for him than any other bachelor in military history. These children included Virginia Pelham Stuart—the last-born child of Pelham's commanding officer, the famous Jeb Stuart.

In March, 1863, Rosser was wounded at Kelly's Ford. In May of that year he married his young lady. It was a sad wedding. Pelham, who was to have been best man, had taken his death wound at Kelly's Ford. In his place stood James Dearing, who would have graduated in 1862 had Virginia stayed in the Union. Before the war ended, Dearing too would be killed in a last futile battle just before Appomattox.

Rosser was one of the few who did not surrender with Lee. He was a major general of cavalry by this time. He had put in almost a year fighting Custer up and down the Shenandoah Valley. Now he tried breaking through to the last Confederate command in the Carolinas. He almost made it. The Yankees caught him near Lynchburg.

So the war was over. Most of his friends were dead, and Tom Rosser was a professional man barred from his profession—a major general with no job and a hungry family. He went to work with a pick and shovel for the Northern Pacific Railroad.

Soon they allowed he was an engineer and gave him the job of surveying the line's route to the West Coast. Regular regiments were assigned to guard these operations from whatever Indians might not like the idea of a railroad so near home.

"Well, I have joined the engineers," wrote Custer to his Elizabeth in 1873. "I was lying half asleep when I heard 'Orderly, which is General Custer's tent?' I sprang up. 'I know that voice, even if I haven't heard it for years!' It was my old friend General Rosser. Stretched on a buffalo robe, under a fly, in the moonlight, we listened to one another's accounts of the battles in which we had been opposed. It seemed like the time when, as cadets, we lay, huddled under one blanket, indulging in dreams of the future." In the weeks to come they refought the old battles and called up the young faces gone forever.

Three years later, when Custer's command was cut off on the Little Big Horn, Rosser prepared to lead a volunteer force to the rescue. Before he could start, word came down the river that it was no use. But Rosser's friendships did not end with life. To the end he defended Custer's reputation.

The day came when Thomas Rosser even renewed his old friendship with the United States. At the outbreak of the Spanish-American War he and two other former Confederate officers—Fitzhugh Lee, class of 1856, and Joseph Wheeler, class of 1859—thought it an excellent example of unity to lead their part of the country back into the blue fighting ranks. Rosser was 61 years old when he received the commission for which he had trained in his youth—brigadier general, *United States Army*.

"There were veterans down our way," writes a native of Alabama, "who were considerably shaken by the event. I remember one old fellow saying, 'I'm a Confederate, and a Christian, and I always aimed to live right, so's I'd go to Heaven. But if them newspapers ain't lyin', an' this here is true, I ain't so sure. Now I reckon I'd rather go to Hell an' see the Devil rip them blue coats off Tom Rosser and Fitz Lee!'"

It was a short war in '98. General Rosser soon returned to his plantation near Charlottesville, Virginia. He became postmaster of the city. His acres were secured by the money he had earned in his bitter western days right after the old war. He died in 1910 an honored and respected man, his children and grandchildren about him, his country unified, happy, and at peace.

Fates more terrible awaited some. Perhaps there were boys in gray who died in Union prison camps in the very state where they had gone to school. It is hard to trace these young southerners. Once a man had resigned, the old records usually cut off his career with the bitter words, "Joined in the rebellion against the United States." Occasionally, if he were killed while "in rebellion," that grim fact is noted. So died at Gettysburg William Westwood McCreery, class of 1860,

CONTINUED ON PAGE 86

The LAST STAND of CHIEF JOSEPH

The Nez Percés led the Army a bitter 1,300-mile chase; when they

surrendered, one of the last free Indian nations vanished into history

By ALVIN M. JOSEPHY, JR.

Joseph, last chief of the Nez Percés, was photographed in Bismarck, Dakota Territory, after his surrender in 1877. The town gave him a dinner honoring his "bravery and humanity."

In June, 1877, just one year after the Custer debacle, a new and unexpected Indian outbreak flared in the West. To an American public wearied and disgusted with a governmental policy, or lack of policy, that seemed to breed Indian wars, this one, an uprising by formerly peaceful Nez Percés * of Oregon and Idaho, was dramatized by what appeared to be superb Indian generalship. One army detachment after another, officered by veterans of the Civil War, floundered in battle with the hostiles. Western correspondents telegraphed the progress of a great, 1,300-mile fighting retreat by the Indians, swaying popular imagination in behalf of the valiant Nez Percés and their leader, Chief Joseph, who, as handsome and noble in appearance as a Fenimore Cooper Indian, became something of a combined national hero and military genius.

The government received no laurels, either, as the long trail of bitter injustices that had originally driven the Nez Percés to hostility became known. The war, like most Indian troubles, had stemmed from a conflict over land. For centuries the Nez Percés had occupied the high, grassy hills and canyon-scarred plateau

---

* The Nez Percés wore pieces of shell in their noses—hence their name, which is French for "pierced nose." The name, whether used in the singular or plural, is pronounced "nez purse."

The Nez Percés rally before Gibbon's charge at Big Hole. Wanton killing of their women and children by soldiers and mutilation of their dead by the Army's Indian scouts convinced the Nez Percés that all white men were their enemies.

land where Washington, Oregon, and Idaho come together. A strong and intelligent people, they had lived in peace and friendship with the whites ever since the coming of Lewis and Clark in 1805, and it was their proud boast that no member of the tribe had ever killed a white man.

In 1855, as settlers began to appear in their country, the government called on them to cede part of their land. The Nez Percés willingly accepted the confines of a reservation, but five years later gold was discovered on the reserve, miners poured in, and in 1863 the government attempted to reduce the reservation to less than one-fourth of its previous size. Led by a chief named Lawyer, those bands whose homes already lay within the boundaries of the new reservation agreed to sign the treaty. But the other chiefs, representing about two-thirds of the tribe, protested and withdrew from the council without signing.

Among the latter was a prominent old chief named Wellamotkin, father of Chief Joseph and known to the whites as Old Joseph. His band, composed of about sixty males and perhaps twice that number of women and children, had dwelt for generations in the Wallowa Valley in the northeastern corner of Oregon.

Isolated on all sides by formidable natural barriers of high mountain ranges and some of the deepest gorges on the continent, the valley's lush alpine grasslands provided some of the best grazing ground in the Northwest, and settlers were particularly anxious to possess it. Old Joseph's refusal to sign the treaty of 1863, however, clouded the issue of ownership, and though the government announced that Lawyer and the chiefs who had signed had spoken for the whole tribe, binding all Nez Percés to the new reservation, no immediate attempt was made to drive Old Joseph's band from the Wallowa.

As the years went by and Old Joseph's people continued unmolested, it seemed as if their right to the Wallowa had been accepted. But white pressure against its borders increased steadily, and in 1871, as he lay dying, Old Joseph fearfully counseled his son:

"When I am gone, think of your country. You are the chief of these people. They look to you to guide them. Always remember that your father never sold his country. You must stop your ears whenever you are asked to sign a treaty selling your home. A few years more, and the white men will be all around you. They have their eyes on this land. My son, never forget my dying words. This country holds your father's body. Never sell the bones of your father and your mother."

The crisis came soon after Old Joseph's death. Settlers from Oregon's Grande Ronde found a route into the Wallowa and moved in, claiming the Indians' land. Young Joseph protested to the Indian agent on the Nez Percé reservation in Idaho, and an investigation by the Bureau of Indian Affairs resulted in a decision that the Wallowa still belonged legally to the Indians. On June 16, 1873, President Grant formally set aside the Wallowa "as a reservation for the roaming Nez Percé Indians" and ordered the whites to withdraw.

Recognition of their rights brought joy to the Indians. But it was short-lived. The settlers, refusing to move, threatened to exterminate Joseph's people if they didn't leave the valley. In defiance of the presidential order, more whites rolled in by the wagonload. As friction increased, Oregon's governor, Leonard P. Grover, attacked Washington officials for having abandoned the government's position of 1863 and forced the Administration to reverse itself. In 1875 a new and confusing presidential edict reopened the Wallowa to white homesteaders.

The Nez Percés were dismayed. Young Joseph, whom they called Heinmot Tooyalakekt, meaning "Thunder Traveling to Loftier Mountain Heights," counseled patience. He moved the Indian camps from the neighborhood of the settlers and again appealed to the federal authorities. The assistant adjutant general of the Military Department of the Columbia, Major H. Clay Wood, was assigned to make a survey of the conflicting claims, and in his report, forwarded to Washington by his commanding officer, O. O. Howard, the one-armed "Christian" general of the Civil War, stated: "In my opinion, the non-treaty Nez Percés cannot in law be regarded as bound by the treaty of 1863, and insofar as it attempts to deprive them of a right to occupancy of any land, its provisions are null and void. The extinguishment of their title of occupancy contemplated by this treaty is imperfect and incomplete."

At first the government took no action, but as harassment of the Indians continued and the threat increased that they might retaliate with violence, a commission of five members was appointed to meet with the Nez Percés in November, 1876, with authority to make a final settlement of the matter for "the welfare of both whites and Indians."

The commissioners, Howard, Wood, and three eastern civilians, found Joseph a disquieting figure. Only 36 years old, tall and powerfully built, he seemed

At the Cow Island crossing Nez Percé warriors stand gua until their women and children are safely away. Then,

strangely amicable and gentle; yet he bore himself with the quiet strength and dignity of one who stood in awe of no man. And when he spoke, it was with an eloquent logic that nettled the whites, who found themselves resenting their inability to dominate him.

Why, they asked him, did he refuse to give up the Wallowa? He answered by referring to the land as the Mother of the Indians, something that could not be sold or given away. "We love the land," he said. "It is our home."

But, they persisted, Lawyer had signed it away in 1863.

Joseph had a ready reply that embarrassed them. "I believe the old treaty has never been correctly reported," he said. "If we ever owned the land we own it still, for we never sold it. In the treaty councils the commissioners have claimed that our country has been sold to the government. Suppose a white man should come to me and say, 'Joseph, I like your horses, and I want to buy them.' I say to him, 'No, my horses suit me, I will not sell them.' Then he goes to my neighbor,

GILCREASE INSTITUTE OF AMERICAN HISTORY AND ART

*idating—but not harming—the Army guards, they plun-
ed the stores to replenish supplies for the flight ahead.*

and says to him, 'Joseph has some good horses. I want
to buy them but he refuses to sell.' My neighbor answers, 'Pay me the money, and I will sell you Joseph's
horses.' The white man returns to me and says,
'Joseph, I have bought your horses and you must let
me have them.' If we sold our lands to the government, this is the way they were bought."

To all their arguments, Joseph replied with an un-
compromising "No" and when the council ended, the
exasperated commissioners had made no progress with
him. But events were moving against the Indians. The
situation in the Wallowa had grown perilous, and
the commission was under political pressure. Two
excited white men had killed an Indian youth after
mistakenly accusing him of stealing their horses. Joseph had had all he could do to keep his people calm,
and the settlers, fearing an uprising, were arming and
calling for military protection.

To the commissioners, despite the fact that it was
unjust and there was no legal basis for it, there could
be only one decision, and before they left the reserva-

tion headquarters at Lapwai, they rendered it: Unless, within a reasonable time, all the non-treaty Nez
Percés (the other bands that had not signed in 1863,
as well as Joseph's people in the Wallowa) voluntarily
came onto the reservation, *they should be placed there
by force.* General Howard, symbolizing the force that
would be used, signed the report along with the three
easterners. Only Major Wood's name was absent, and
it is believed that he submitted a minority report,
though it has never been found.

Immediately after the decision, the Indian Bureau
defined the "reasonable time" and ordered the Indians
to come onto the reservation by April 1, 1877. Unable
to move their herds and villages across the rugged
canyons in the dead of winter, the Nez Percés appealed for another conference, and, as April 1 came
and went, General Howard agreed to one last meeting
with all the non-treaty chiefs at Lapwai. It did no
good. The die had been cast, and Howard adamantly
refused to discuss the commission's decision. As the
Indians pleaded in proud but pitiable terms to be allowed to remain in the lands where their fathers were
buried, the General finally lost patience and threw
one of the most respected old chiefs, a deeply religious
war leader and tribal orator named Toohoolhoolzote,
into the guardhouse. It broke the spirit of the others.
To gain Toohoolhoolzote's release, they capitulated
with bitterness and agreed to have their bands on the
reservation in thirty days.

All of Joseph's skill as a diplomat had to be called
into play when he returned to his people. He had
abandoned his father's counsel and trust, and there
were cries to ignore him and go to war rather than to
move to the reservation. When Joseph argued that the
white man's power was too great for them to resist and
that it was "better to live at peace than to begin a war
and lie dead," they called him a coward. But he received strong assistance from his younger brother,
Ollokot, a daring and courageous buffalo hunter and
warrior who had won many tribal honors and held
the respect of the more belligerent younger element.
Eventually the two brothers won agreement to the
capitulation from the band's council. With heavy
hearts, the Indians prepared to round up their stock
and move.

A half year's work was crowded into less than thirty
days as the people combed the mountains and forests
for their animals and drove them down the steep
draws to the Snake. The river was in flood, and hundreds of head of stock were swept away and drowned
during the tumultuous crossing. Other portions of the
herds, left behind on the bluffs and plateau, were
driven away by whites who attacked the guards and
harassed the withdrawing Indians. By June 2, with

twelve days of grace remaining, the people reached an ancient tribal rendezvous area just outside the border of the reservation. Here they joined the other non-treaty bands and lingered for a last bit of freedom.

It was a fatal pause. On June 12 the Indians staged a parade through the camp, and one of the young men named Wahlitits, whose father had been murdered by a white man two years before, was taunted by an old warrior for having allowed the slaying to go unavenged. The next morning, his honor as a man impugned, Wahlitits stole away with two companions. By nightfall, in an outpouring of long-suppressed hatred, the youths had killed four white men along the Salmon River and wounded another one, all notorious for their hostility to the Nez Percés. The young men returned to the camp, announced what they had done, and raised a bigger party that continued the raids during the next two days, killing fourteen or fifteen additional whites and striking terror among the settlers and miners of central Idaho.

Both Joseph and Ollokot had been absent from the camp during the first raid, butchering cattle on the opposite side of the Salmon River. They returned in horror, finding the camp in confusion and the older people crying with fear and striking their tepees, intending to scatter to hiding places. Most of the Indians were certain that there would now be war, but Joseph still hoped to avert it. He tried to calm his people, assuring them that General Howard would not blame the whole tribe for the irresponsible actions of a few of its young hotheads, and urged them to remain where they were and await the troops, with whom he would make a settlement. The situation, however, had gone too far. The warriors rode around the camp, crying out that they would now give General Howard the fight that he had wanted, and the people would not listen to Joseph. One by one the bands departed to a hiding place farther south, in White Bird Canyon, leaving behind only Joseph, Ollokot, and a few of the Wallowa Indians.

Joseph's wife had given birth to a daughter while he had been across the Salmon, and he lingered with her now in their tepee. Several warriors were detailed to watch him and Ollokot, lest these leaders who had so often pleaded for peace would desert the non-treaties and move onto the reservation. But though he had vigorously opposed war, Joseph would not abandon his people; two days later he and Ollokot, resolved to fight now that hostilities seemed unavoidable, joined the non-treaties in the new camp at White Bird.

Back at Lapwai Howard was stunned by news of the Salmon River outbreaks. He had planned all winter against trouble in the Wallowa, and when Jo-seph had moved out peacefully, he had thought that all danger was past. At the news of the outbreaks, he hastily ordered two troops of the 1st Cavalry, that had been stationed at Lapwai, ninety troopers and four officers under Captain David Perry and Captain Joel Trimble, to round up the hostiles and force them onto the reservation. Eleven civilian volunteers and twelve treaty Nez Percés accompanied the troops, and after a rapid two days' march of almost eighty miles, they learned of the Nez Percé camp in White Bird Canyon and prepared to attack it early the following morning.

Alert Indian spies warned the Nez Percés of the troops' approach. The soldiers would have to descend a long draw of treeless, rolling land, flanked by ridges and hills, to reach the Nez Percé village, which lay behind two buttes at the bottom of the slope. The chiefs were uncertain whether to resist and detailed six men to take a flag of truce forward and try to arrange a peaceful meeting with the officers. At the same time, the old men, women, and children were ordered to drive in the camp's stock, while the warriors, stripping for action and mounting their ponies, sought hiding places to the right and left of the draw to await events. The total manpower of the Indian bands was about 150, but many of the men that morning were lying in camp, drunk on whisky seized during the raids and unable to fight. Others had no weapons or were too old, sick, or frightened to use them. Altogether, not more than 45 or 50 Indians—armed with bows and arrows; shotguns; old, muzzle-loading, fur-trade muskets; and a few modern rifles—rode out to defend the village.

The nature of the terrain, offering a multitude of hiding places for flanking attacks, should have put the troopers on their guard. Instead they trotted confidently down the draw, ready for a thundering surprise charge. As they rounded a small hill, the Indian truce team appeared directly ahead of them. Behind the men with the white flag were other Nez Percés, sitting on their horses waiting to see what would happen. There was an instant of surprise. Then a volunteer raised his rifle and shot at the truce team. The Indians backed away, unharmed, a Nez Percé behind them fired in return, killing one of Perry's two trumpeters, and the fight was on. As Indians began shooting from all directions, Perry hastily deployed his men in a line across the draw, placing the volunteers on a high, rocky knoll to his left. The company in the center dismounted, letting men in the rear hold their horses, and the company on the right remained mounted.

The battle, fought without plan by the Indians, lasted only a few moments. On the left a small body of Nez Percés swept from behind a hill and galloped straight at the volunteers, sending them flying in panic back up the draw and exposing Perry's whole line. At the same time Ollokot, leading a large number of warriors, emerged from cover on the right and, firing as he came, charged into Perry's mounted troop, frightening the horses and disorganizing the soldiers. The men in the center, seeing Indians and confusion all around them, gave way and made a sudden rush for their horses. In a few minutes the entire command was cut into small groups fighting desperately for their lives. Nineteen men under Lieutenant Edward Theller tried to make a stand but were driven against a rocky wall and wiped out. The rest of the troop disintegrated into a fleeing rabble and got away, leaving behind them a total of 34 dead, a third of Perry's command. The Indians had only two men wounded and none killed; equally important for the future, they retrieved from the battlefield 63 rifles and a large number of pistols.

Perry's defeat spread alarm throughout the settlements of the Northwest and angered the rest of the nation, to whom the Custer massacre was still fresh. Howard was shocked and, fearing that the uprising would spread to the treaty Nez Percés as well as other Northwest tribes, called for troop reinforcements from all over the West. Men were started inland from Portland and San Francisco, artillerymen returning from Alaska were diverted up the Columbia, and from as far away as Atlanta, Georgia, infantry units were entrained for the scene of the new Indian outbreak.

Within a week Howard himself took the field. With a force of 227 hastily assembled troops, 20 civilians, and a large group of packers and guides, he marched hurriedly out from Lapwai, intending to punish the hostiles. The Indians, reinforced by a small band that had just returned from the Montana buffalo plains under the leadership of two redoubtable warriors, Five Wounds and Rainbow, had withdrawn from White Bird and, when Howard caught up with them, had crossed with all their equipment and pony herds to the relative safety of the south bank of the Salmon. For a while the two groups faced each other from opposite sides of the wilderness river while Howard planned how to get his troops across the turbulent stream and catch the Indians before they could retreat into the rocky wilds of central Idaho. From his rear he received false information from excited settlers that a large band of hitherto peaceful Nez Percés, under a famous tribal war chief named Looking Glass, was planning to leave the reservation and join the hostiles. Accepting the information as true, he divided his forces and sent Captain Stephen Whipple with two troops of cavalry to intercept Looking Glass.

It was a disastrous move. As Whipple departed,

Looking Glass astride a painted horse was photographed by W. H. Jackson in 1871. One of the tribe's most important war chiefs, he was elected head of the non-treaty group. The Nez Percés decorated their horses as well as themselves.

Howard received boats and started across the river, only to see the Indians move off into the wilderness ahead of him. For several days he was led on a wearying, frustrating chase through mud and driving rain, up and down steep hills and mountain slopes, and across some of the most rugged terrain in the West. Meanwhile Whipple reached Looking Glass's village on the reservation and, although he found it peaceful, launched a vicious assault upon it. The startled Indians, struck without warning, fled across a river to the shelter of some trees, where they were rallied by their outraged chief. Rumors now came to Whipple that the main band of Indians had somehow evaded General Howard, had recrossed the Salmon, and were between him and the General, threatening his own rear, Howard's supply lines, and all the settlements on the Camas Prairie which he was supposed to be protecting.

The rumors this time were true. With Howard's troops floundering in the wilds, the non-treaties had managed to cross again to the north side of the Salmon. Howard tried to follow them, couldn't get his men and equipment across the river, and had to go back over the entire dreadful mountain trail to the place of his original crossing, where he had left his boats. Meanwhile Whipple, forgetting Looking Glass in the face of the full Nez Percé force, sent out a reconnoitering party of ten men under Lieutenant S. M. Rains and dug in for an expected attack. The Indians wiped out Rains's party to a man, cut up another group of scouts and several hastily formed bodies of civilian volunteers, and finally, bypassing Whipple and the terrified settlers barricaded in Cottonwood and Grangeville, moved to another hiding place on the South Fork of the Clearwater River. Here they were joined by Looking Glass's infuriated band. It gave the Indians another forty fighting men but also raised the number of women and children, who would have to be carried along and protected from the soldiers, to a peak figure of 450.

A colorfully beaded Nez Percé breastplate, worn for decoration.

From the beginning it had been assumed by the whites that Joseph, spokesman for the non-treaties in peacetime, had also been leading them in war. Howard had credited him with skillfully contriving the ambush of Perry at White Bird. Now Joseph was being given grudging praise for the masterful way in which the Indians had evaded Howard in the wilderness and doubled back to get between him and Whipple. In addition, the Nez Percés had been conducting themselves in an unusual manner for Indians "on the warpath," refraining from scalping or mutilating bodies, treating white women and noncombatants with humanity and even friendliness, and otherwise adhering to what was considered the white man's code of war. This too was credited to Joseph, whose dignity and decency at prewar councils were recalled by Howard and the Indian agents.

The truth was that Nez Percé successes were resulting from a combination of overconfidence and mistakes on the part of the whites, the rugged terrain that made pursuit difficult, and, to a very great extent, the Indians' intense courage and patriotic determination to fight for their rights and protect their people. Indian strategy and tactics had also played a role, but at each step of the way these were agreed upon in coun-

cils of all the chiefs and were carried out on the field by the younger war leaders and their warriors. Joseph sat in the councils, but since he had never been a war chief his advice carried less weight than that of men like Five Wounds, Toohoolhoolzote, and Rainbow. On the march and in battle Joseph took charge of the old men, women, and children, an assignment of vital importance and sacred trust, while Ollokot and the experienced war chiefs led the young men on guard duty or in combat. The whites had no way of knowing this, and, as events continued to unfold, the legend that Nez Percé strategy was planned and executed by one man, Joseph, was spread far and wide by the hapless army officers opposing him and accepted without question by correspondents and the U.S. public.

On July 11, with a reinforced army of 400 soldiers and 180 scouts, packers, and teamsters, Howard was back in pursuit of the Nez Percés. Suddenly he sighted their camp lying below him on the opposite side of the Clearwater River, opened fire with a four-inch howitzer and two Gatling guns, and prepared to launch an attack. The Nez Percés were taken by surprise, but old Toohoolhoolzote and 24 warriors raced across the river, scaled a bluff to the level of the soldiers, and, taking shelter behind boulders, engaged the troopers with a fierce and accurate fire that held them up until more Indians could come across and get into the fight. The firing was sharp on both sides, but as increasing numbers of mounted Nez Percés began appearing over the top of the bluff to circle the troops' rear and flanks, Howard hastened his men into a square and ordered them to dig in on the open, rocky ground with their trowel bayonets.

The fighting raged all day and continued in the same spot the next morning, an almost unprecedented length of time for Indians to maintain battle in one location. The Nez Percés, outnumbered almost six to one and occasionally under artillery fire, kept the troopers pinned down and on the defensive with marksmanship that Howard's adjutant, Major C. E. S. Wood, described as "terribly accurate and very fatal." Several times small groups of Indians darted forward to engage the soldiers in hand-to-hand fights, and once they almost captured Howard's supply train. In addition, the Nez Percés held the only spring in the area and controlled access to the river; under the blazing July sun the soldiers suffered unmercifully from thirst.

By noon of the second day the chiefs had decided that there had been enough fighting without decision. Many of the warriors had become restless and tired and wanted to leave. Holding the line long enough for Joseph to get the families packed and safely away with the herds, the Indians, one by one, ceased fighting and withdrew down the bluff. Howard's troops followed the last of them across the river and through the abandoned camp. It was an anticlimactic and hollow finish to a battle that had cost the army thirteen killed and twenty-seven wounded, two of them fatally. Howard could count four Indians killed and six wounded, but the hostiles had escaped from him again.

The Nez Percés crossed the Clearwater north of the troops and paused at an old meeting ground on the Weippe Prairie to decide what to do next. They had had enough of Howard and thought that if they left Idaho and went somewhere else, the General would be satisfied and would leave them alone. Looking Glass, who many times had hunted buffalo and fought with the Crows in Montana, urged that they cross the mountains and join that tribe. They could then hunt on the plains in peace, he told them, and the war would be over. It was a harsh proposal, for it meant the final abandonment of their homeland, but with the people's safety weighing heavily on them Joseph and the other chiefs reluctantly agreed to the exodus. On July 16, having named Looking Glass as supreme chief for the trek to the Crows, the bands set off on the arduous Lolo Trail across the wild and precipitous heights of the Bitterroot Mountains.

Smarting under increasing criticism from Washington, as well as from the press and public, Howard once more took after the Indians, doggedly following their trail up through the thick and tangled forest growth of mountain slopes to the high, ridge-top route that led

CONTINUED ON PAGE 78

Walking slowly toward General Howard and Colonel Miles, Joseph raises his arm in salute and accepts the honorable terms given him. Over the protests of Howard and Miles, the government promptly violated the agreement.

43

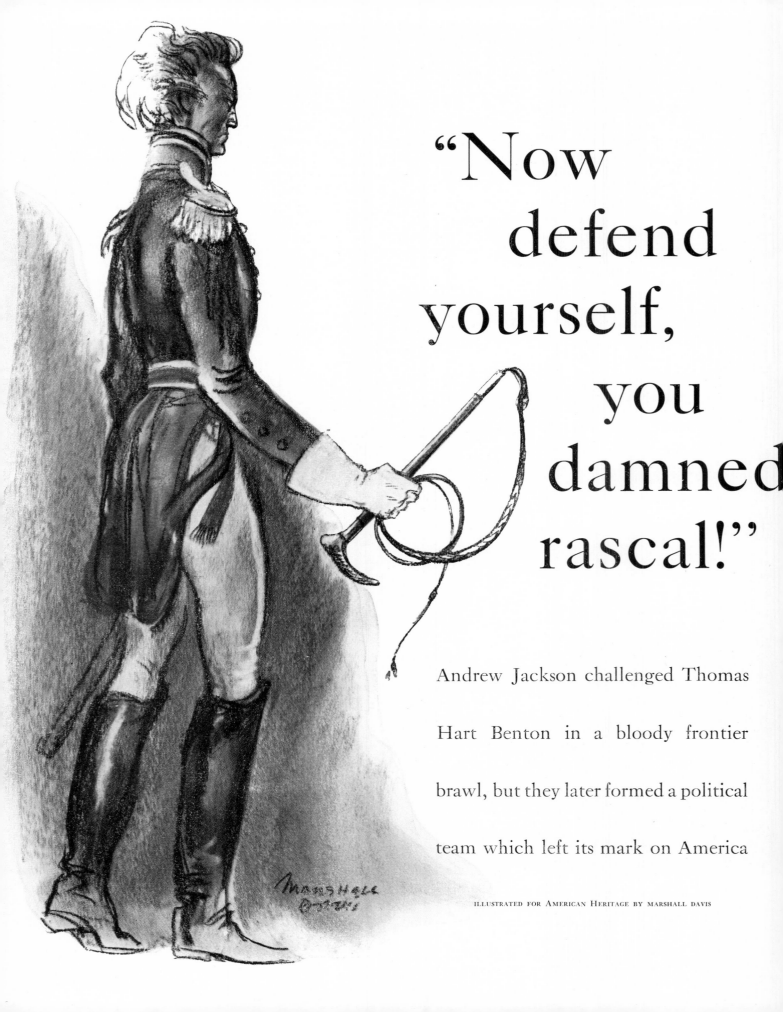

"Now defend yourself, you damned rascal!"

Andrew Jackson challenged Thomas Hart Benton in a bloody frontier brawl, but they later formed a political team which left its mark on America

ILLUSTRATED FOR AMERICAN HERITAGE BY MARSHALL DAVIS

As the chanting of his slaves announced the approaching death of Andrew Jackson, on a June day in 1845, the old warrior spent part of his last conscious moments dictating farewell messages to men whose love he had valued—Francis P. Blair, Sam Houston, and Thomas Hart Benton. The appearance of Benton on this list was natural, for he had become the old general's most devoted partisan; but thirty years earlier it would have caused great surprise, for Benton and Jackson had been the bitterest of enemies and had once tried their level best to kill one another. The strange duel they fought—it took place during the War of 1812—was one of the odd landmarks of American political history.

By ELBERT B. SMITH

The two had become acquainted shortly before that war began. Jackson was the elder by fifteen years, and his famous fight with Benton was only one of a number of violent episodes in his long career. He had fought two duels (one of which ended fatally for his opponent), had caned various enemies, and had sent numerous challenges that went unaccepted. He tangled twice with Governor John Sevier of Tennessee, once trading shots with him in a crowd—a slightly wounded bystander was the only casualty—and once meeting him more formally, but very anticlimactically, on the dueling ground; Sevier's horse ran away with the pistols, and both men were led away, swearing at each other until out of earshot. Benton also had a high temper. At sixteen he had initiated a pistol duel with a schoolmate, and only the vigilance of a professor had averted bloodshed.

Physically, the two men were in contrast. Jackson was tall and thin; the irreverent said that he was skinny. Equally tall, Benton was built along the general lines of a modern professional football tackle—broad, thick, and heavily muscled. In education and intellect, Benton was the superior; in capacity for blind fury, utter recklessness, and iron-willed determination, neither man had a superior.

As so often happened in that era of hot tempers and the violent settlement of disputes, their famous duel grew out of a close friendship.

Shortly before the beginning of the War of 1812, Benton was a struggling young attorney, cursed by ill health. His father and three sisters had died of tuberculosis, and Benton himself, suffering from a fever and a racking cough, saw his own end at hand. But the arrival of the war with England brought him a chance to escape from obscurity and ill health alike. In February, 1812, when war seemed imminent, he conceived a plan for recruiting three regiments of volunteers and rode off through thirty miles of rain and mud to present it in person at the Hermitage. Jackson was impressed; with Benton's help he raised a force of more than 2,000 men and by early January, 1813, was leading them down the Cumberland, Ohio, and Mississippi rivers on flatboats to defend New Orleans. Benton was colonel of one of the infantry regiments and doubled as Jackson's principal aide.

Nothing went right—except that the outdoor exercise and fresh air restored Benton's health and ended his apparent predisposition to tuberculosis. At Natchez the War Department punctured the leaders' dreams of glory by ordering Jackson to disband his army and turn all public property over to General James Wilkinson. Jackson flatly refused to let his men join Wilkinson's regulars and announced that he would lead them home on his own responsibility. Benton stuck with him, although he did say that Wilkinson was legally his superior and that if he were ordered to take his regiment and fight under him he could not refuse. As it happened, this did not become an issue.

Back to Nashville, 800 inglorious miles, went the volunteers. Jackson had spent a good deal of his own money on the expedition, and he needed reimbursement; it was agreed that Benton would go to Washington and present his claims. This Benton did, winning governmental approval of Jackson's expense vouchers and incidentally wangling a commission as lieutenant colonel in the Regular Army for himself. But during his absence there was a development that led to an abrupt souring of the friendship between the two men.

A challenge for a duel had passed between two officers in Jackson's army, Major William Carroll and Ensign Lyttleton Johnston; Benton's younger brother, Jesse, was acting as Ensign Johnston's second. Andrew Jackson intervened to make peace, but peacemaking was never Old Hickory's long suit, and while the original cause of action did get settled Jesse Benton somehow became involved in an argument with Major Carroll and wound up committed to fight a duel with him. And Major Carroll's second was Jackson himself.

The actual duel turned out to be a fiasco that gave Tennesseeans cause for laughter for years to come. Carroll was a notoriously poor shot with a pistol; therefore it was arranged that the duelists would stand back to back, ten feet apart, and on the signal would wheel and fire. Jesse Benton protested these arrangements—which seem to have been devised by Jackson—but got nowhere. When the duel was fought, he wheeled in a squatting position in order to reduce the target area—and promptly got a painful wound in the seat of his pants.

Thomas Hart Benton returned to Tennessee, learned of all of this, and concluded that Jackson had not acted as an old friend should. He said as much, Jackson heard about it, and presently Jackson sent Benton an ominously calm note asking about it: Had Benton been complaining, and, specifically, was there any truth in the rumor that he had threatened to send Jackson a challenge?

Benton sent an outspoken reply. He did not think much of Jackson's actions in connection with the various quarrels, he thought the duel had been conducted in a "savage, unequal, unfair, and base manner," and all in all he did not like any of it. He would not challenge, but the threat of the General's pistols would not seal his lips. He would continue to speak the truth, neither seeking nor declining a duel.

No man could write to Old Hickory that way without getting a vigorous reply. Jackson wrote angrily: "It is the character of the man of honor, and particularly of the *soldier,* not to quarrel and brawl like fish women." He defended everything he had done and announced flatly that Benton should either admit error or demand satisfaction.

Inevitably, for neither Jackson nor Benton ever reacted in a halfway manner, this led to a duel. Yet the duel that at last was fought bore no resemblance to the formal, courtly affairs specified in the romantic code. Rather, it looked more like an outright frontier brawl, utterly without formalities: a savage collision between two angry men each determined to do the other all the bodily harm possible.

After the exchange of letters between Jackson and Benton, talebearers continued their work until Jackson announced that he would horsewhip Tom Benton on sight. His opportunity finally came on September 4, 1813, when the Benton brothers arrived in Nashville on business. They stayed at a hotel not frequented by Jackson in order, in Benton's words, to avoid "a possibility of unpleasantness." Word of their presence spread quickly, and soon Jackson, Colonel John Coffee, and Stockley Hays arrived at the Nashville Inn. Both Coffee and Hays were gigantic men, a fit palace guard for their smaller but more aggressive leader. Each of the Bentons carried two pistols. The Jackson war party was equally well armed, and in addition Jackson, meaning to fulfill his pledge, carried a riding whip.

Jackson and Coffee first strolled to the post office, passing near Talbot's tavern, where the Bentons were standing on the walk. Returning the same way, they saw Jesse Benton step from the pavement into the hotel. Jackson unhesitatingly assumed the role of aggressor by following Jesse into the hotel. Jesse had disappeared, but Thomas was standing in the doorway of the hall leading to the rear porch. Brandishing the whip, Jackson advanced upon Thomas Benton: "Now defend yourself, you damned rascal!" Benton reached for his pistol, but Jackson's draw was quicker. Looking into the muzzle of Jackson's pistol, Thomas Benton slowly retreated, with Jackson following step by step. Jesse Benton, meanwhile, slipped through a doorway behind Jackson, raised his gun, and fired. At the same moment, Jackson fired twice at Thomas Benton, who fired back twice in return. Jackson fell with his left shoulder shattered and a ball imbedded in his arm. The blast from Jackson's gun had burned a hole in Thomas Benton's sleeve. At this moment tall John Coffee came charging through the smoke, fired at Thomas Benton, missed, and attacked with the butt of his pistol. Fortunately the carnage was limited by the fact that the Colt six-shooter had not yet been invented; the fire-belching smoothbore pistols the antagonists used were not particularly accurate and, once fired, were useless. Jackson's friends, however, by now reinforced, almost finished their leader's mission. Wielding daggers, Coffee and Alexander Donelson managed to wound Thomas Benton in five places. Stockley Hays stabbed away at Jesse with a sword cane, and only a large and strong button which broke Hays' blade saved Jesse from being perforated. Jesse placed the muzzle of his remaining pistol against Hays' chest and pulled the trigger, but in a fair exchange of mishaps the charge failed to explode. Thomas Benton, meanwhile, in his efforts to parry the dagger thrusts of Coffee and Donelson, fell backward down a flight of stairs. The obviously serious plight of the bleeding Jackson brought the melee to an end. Friends carried the General back to his hotel, where he soaked two mattresses with blood. An ordinary man would have died, but iron-willed Andrew Jackson had not yet decided to expire. He had been defeated, however, and battered Thomas Benton sealed the victory by breaking Jackson's sword across his knee in the public square.

Fighting one's commander was no step to fame. Thomas Benton still hungered for military glory, but the battle with Jackson was to be his only victory in the War of 1812. Benton was an excellent recruiting officer, and Jackson used this fact for a subtle revenge. On the eve of the great Battle of Horseshoe Bend and again just before his final march to immortality at New Orleans, Jackson ordered the Colonel back to Nashville for recruiting. On the second occasion Benton pleaded for a chance to fight as a private in the ranks, but Old Hickory was adamant. Wishing to see his other "brave officers at the head of their respective commands where fresh laurels await them, and finding that they cannot fill their companies here," the General stood by his order. Benton finally wangled an assignment to Canada, but it came after the peace treaty and Jackson's victory at New Orleans. Leaving the army early in 1815, Benton could see only a blighted future as long as he remained in the same state with Jackson, so he decided to seek out a new career in the vast land beyond the Mississippi.

In December, 1823, almost ten years later, the newly elected Senator Andrew Jackson of Tennessee arrived at the capitol to take the one conspicuously vacant seat in the Senate chamber. Next to him sat Senator Thomas Hart Benton of Missouri, if anything bigger and more irritatingly self-assured than ever. They had not met since 1813. Fearing a possible explosion, several senators offered to exchange seats with them, but both men declined, taking no notice of each other.

The air about the two savage lawmakers remained charged for several days until they were assigned to the same committee with Jackson as chairman. Old Hickory finally broke the ice. Facing Benton squarely one day, he said, "Colonel, we are on the same committee; I will give you notice when it is necessary to attend."

The younger man was equal to the occasion: "General, make the time to suit yourself." After a session in committee together they exchanged queries as to the health of their respective wives, and a few days later Jackson left his card at the Benton lodgings: "Andrew Jackson for Colonel Benton and lady." Finally Colonel and Mrs. Benton found themselves with Senator Jackson at a White House dinner. Benton made the first bow, accepted Jackson's extended hand, and introduced Mrs. Benton. Civil relations were restored.

Shortly afterward Senator John Eaton wrote the always-worried Mrs. Jackson a reassuring letter: The General was now reconciled with his enemies, including "what you would never have expected, Col. Benton." Jackson himself added a benign postscript: "It is a pleasing subject to me that I am now at peace with all the world."

Peace, however, was not a normal state for Andrew Jackson, and it did not continue long enough to affect his character seriously. Running for President in 1824, the General received more popular votes than any other candidate but not the required majority of the

CONTINUED ON PAGE 106

In the Low Country of South Carolina,

English and Huguenot planters raised

up a prosperous American city-state

with a high culture and a lasting charm

The Charleston Tradition

By ANTHONY HARRIGAN

These charming paintings of Charleston were done in 1831 by a little-known visiting artist named S. Bernard. At top, he viewed the city and its busy harbor from the Cooper River. The fort is Castle Pinckney, on the tiny island called Shute's Folly. In the lower painting, the Cooper is seen from the prosperous water-front section called the East Battery. Some of the buildings pictured here still stand, as does High Battery, the elevated promenade along the river's edge.

We wish to express our appreciation to the executive board and to the staff of the Gibbes Art Gallery at Charleston. All illustrations which accompany this article, unless otherwise credited, are reproduced through the courtesy of the Carolina Art Association, which maintains the Gibbes Gallery.

From the beginning, Charleston was different. Lord Anthony Ashley Cooper, chief among the Lords Proprietors, planned it that way. For his "darling," as he called the settlement, he had philosopher John Locke prepare Fundamental Constitutions designed to avoid "a too numerous democracy." This frontier province, the future Earl of Shaftesbury hoped, would be a bulwark of the aristocratic principle in government, a New World version of the England of gentlemen seated on their estates.

In this image was Charleston created by Lord Ashley, the brilliant, suffering genius whose life depended on a gold tube draining a cyst in his liver. Thus begun as a citadel of faith in the primacy of excellence over numbers—on a continent which was to be dedicated to the proposition that all men are created equal—Charleston played a unique role in American life until Sherman's Army of the West swept across the Carolinas in 1865.

The city ordained by Lord Ashley was unique in another respect. Alone among the old cities on the eastern seaboard, Charleston—or Charles Town as it was originally named—was a city-state, a South Atlantic Venice built on mud, cribs of palmetto logs loaded with cobblestone ballast, sawdust, and the wastes of a frontier community, diked and protected against hurricane tides with sea walls of crushed oyster shell known as tabby.

The first settlers sailed from England in August of 1669 aboard three small vessels, the *Carolina*, the *Port*

Royal, and the *Albemarle.* The vessels, ranging from 200 to 300 tons, weighed anchor six years after Charles II had given to eight of his loyal supporters "all that territory . . . called Carolina scituate, lying, and being within our dominions of America, extending from the north end of the island called Lucke Island, which lieth in the Southern Virginia seas . . . and to the west as far as the South Seas and so southerly as far as the River Mathias which borderth upon the coast of Florida . . ."

The settlers—some 150 of them—reached the west bank of what is today the Ashley River, across from present-day Charleston.

At this location, Albemarle Point, the settlers lived and suffered for ten years. They might have been massacred, as other settlers were in those grim days, had it not been for one of their number, a surgeon named Henry Woodward. Five years before he had been a member of an earlier Carolina settlement at Cape Fear, and in the interim he had lived for a time among the coastal Indians to learn their language. As interpreter, go-between, and Indian agent, Woodward was an indispensable aid to the settlers of Albemarle Point and, later, of Charleston itself.

One year after Albemarle Point was settled, it was proposed that a new settlement be established across the river on the peninsula between the Kiawah and Etiwan rivers, which had been renamed Ashley and Cooper. Joseph Dalton, a member of the Grand Council, wrote Lord Ashley concerning the proposed site: "It is as it were a Key to open and shutt this settlement into safety or danger; Charles Towne [Albemarle Point] indeed can very well defend itself and thats all, but that [the proposed site] like an Iron gate shutts up all the towns that are or may be in those Rivers."

As Dalton went on to say, the city's approaches from the sea are unique. As one traveler was to observe in the nineteenth century, one yields readily to the illusion that the city springs directly from the bosom of

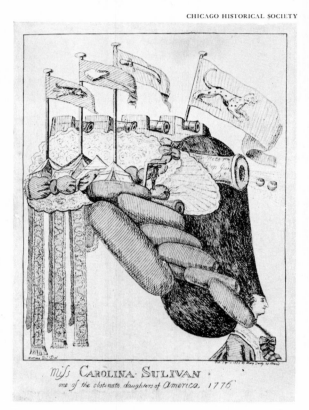

A contemporary London engraver satirized the defeat of the British fleet at Sullivan's Island in 1776 in terms of the exaggerated coiffure of the time.

the waves. The location of the city, at the meeting place of two great rivers, gave rise quite naturally to the ancient witticism that "the Ashley and Cooper Rivers come together to form the Atlantic Ocean."

The physical location of a city has an influence on its character. Charleston's bold front to the sea, where the worst lashings of tide and storm are felt, may have had some part in the shaping of the city's outlook on life. As for the "Iron gate" referred to by Councilman Dalton, the fleets of Spain, France, England, and the Union were to try to batter their way through and almost always they would fail.

But a city is more than an image in the mind of its founder and a meaningful location. It is the people who settle it, and these were a hardy lot, men of parts, rugged individualists. Some 500 English Dissenters came to the city soon after it was established on its present site. To groups of bold thinkers the religious toleration granted by the Proprietors was a spur to emigration. There were planters from the Barbados in the final year of the 1670's. (There were also Negro slaves from the West Indies, and thus one basic feature of the settlement was established early.) Charleston was an English community, but English colonial, almost West Indian in many ways. Presently others came—Scotsmen, Congregationalists from Massachusetts, Quakers, Sephardic Jews; but the most notable event was the arrival in 1680 of the ship *Richmond* with the first contingent of French Huguenots, men and women whose descendants were to play an important role in the city.

The Huguenots had fled their homeland after the Revocation of the Edict of Nantes deprived them of their right to be Protestants at home. They were admitted because the Proprietors wanted people "skilled in yᵉ manufacture of silkes, oyles, wines, &c." Soon they outgrew the role assigned them, and their names —Laurens, Poinsett, Legaré—are on every page of Charleston's history from 1680 to the present day.

TEXT CONTINUED ON PAGE 88

The Revolution: one victory, one defeat

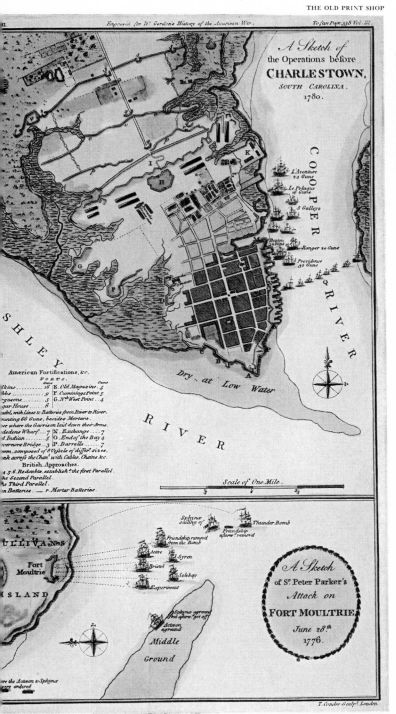

*Two Charleston patriots who became promi-
nent in the new American nation were the
Pinckney brothers, Charles Cotesworth (top)
and Thomas. Gentlemen born and bred,
they were educated at Oxford and made the
Grand Tour. During the Revolution they
campaigned in the South until both were
taken prisoner by the British. Later, Thomas
was minister to England and to Spain in
Washington's Administration. His brother
served as minister to France and twice received the Federalist presidential nomination.*

*These maps outline the major Revolutionary battles around
Charleston. On June 28, 1776, nine British warships shelled
Moultrie's small fort on Sullivan's Island (lower panel) but
were repulsed, badly battered. Four years later (above) the
British (red line) won a great victory; 5,000 Americans
trapped in the city surrendered to Sir Henry Clinton's army.*

*This portrait of William Moultrie, the hero
of Sullivan's Island and twice governor of
South Carolina, is attributed to C. W. Peale.*

51

Low Country high life

1. Honᵇˡᵉ Peter Manigault
2. Taylor, an Officer
3. Demaré — do —
4. Capᵗⁿ Massey

Mʳ Peter Manigault and his Friends,
Drawn by One of them (Mʳ Roupell) about the year 1754 from which this Copy is now made in August 1854
By his Great-Grand-Son Louis Manigault
Charleston So. Ca.

5. Mʳ Isaac Godin
6. Coytmore, an Officer
7. Colⁿ Probart Howarth
8. Mʳ George Roupell

Gabriel Manigault

A spirited gathering at the table of Peter Manigault, a wealthy merchant who was a third-generation Huguenot, was drawn by one of the party, George Roupell, and re-copied years later by a descendant of Manigault. The dialogue, as recorded by Roupell, appears below; the speakers are numbered clockwise, beginning with Manigault (1):

PETER MANIGAULT (1): *"Your toast, Howarth."*
TAYLOR, an officer (2): *"Hey to the Midnight! Hark a-way! Hark a-way!"*
DEMARE, an officer (3): *"Success to Caroline. G – – d damn!"*
CAPTAIN MASSEY (4): *"This one bumper, dear Isaac?"*
MR. ISAAC CODIN (5): *"I shall be drunk, I tell you, Massey."*
COYTMORE, an officer (6): *"Whose toast is it?"*
COLONEL HOWARTH (7): *"Squire Isaac, your wig, you dog."*
MR. GEORGE ROUPELL (8): *"Pray less noise, Gentlemen."*

Another convivial scene is depicted in this stained 1827 wash drawing by Thomas Middleton, a planter who was an amateur artist of no small ability. Middleton (standing at center, flute in hand) described whimsically how "a number of gentlemen friends and amateurs in musick, frequently met at each others houses . . . to beguile away the time in listening to the soothing strains of their own music—I have to apologize for certain glass . . . on the table, but it was Vain to remonstrate." The serious tone of this musicale is exemplified by the gentleman at far right who is imitating a bass violin on a guitar case.

In 1802 a young artist named Charles Fraser did this water color of Steepbrook, one of several Manigault rice plantations. It had been built by Peter Manigault in the 1750's; and here occurred the stag party shown on the opposite page. When Fraser made his sketch, the estate's owner was Peter's son Gabriel (opposite page), a successful planter-architect.

This double portrait of rice and indigo planter *Ralph Izard* and his wife, *Alice DeLancey*, was painted by John Singleton Copley in 1775. Of Huguenot descent, Izard was a wealthy and cultivated man who much preferred the refined atmosphere of England and the Continent to his native city. It was during a stay in Rome that he commissioned the noted American artist to do the picture. But Izard never brought it back to Charleston, for the Revolution cut off a large part of his Carolina income, and he was unable to pay Copley.

Standing in a jungle of live oaks and second-growth timber are the ruins of the Izard family plantation, *The Elms*. It was built in 1810 by Ralph Izard's son Henry on the site of an eighteenth-century mansion which had been destroyed by fire. Situated on a Cooper River tributary called Goose Creek, it was close to the Manigaults' *Steepbrook*. Ironically, the house survived the depredations of Sherman's rampaging columns, only to be so badly damaged in an earthquake which struck in 1886 that it had to be abandoned.

Two famous families of Charleston

The children in this 1817 miniature, Ralph Stead Izard and his sister Anne, represented the seventh generation of their family in South Carolina. The lady on the cover of this issue was their aunt, and their mother was the grand-daughter of Peter Manigault, host at the dinner party on page 52. They are distant cousins of the Izards on the opposite page. Young Ralph was educated abroad, spent several years in foreign travel and returned home to become an able and prosperous rice planter in his own right.

Another rich Charlestonian, Charles Izard Manigault, sat for a fashionable Roman portrait painter with his wife and two small sons while on a tour of Europe in 1831. Charles was the son of Gabriel Manigault and the grandson of Ralph Izard of the Copley painting. Inheriting his father's many estates, he had further augmented his wealth in the China trade; thus he was able to spend much of his life traveling abroad. It was Charles Izard Manigault who finally brought the portrait of his grandparents back to Charleston, paying Copley's widow the fifty-guinea bill which had been overdue for more than fifty years.

Mrs. Henry Broughton Mazyck

Belles and beaux on ivory

These are the faces of Charleston's aristocracy in the early nineteenth century, painted on ivory by such famous miniaturists as Edward Greene Malbone and Charles Fraser (below, right), a talented Charlestonian who executed seven of these delicately wrought portraits. Members of a small, select society closely knit by intermarriage, most of these nineteen people were of English or Scotch blood, though eight of them were Huguenots. Marriage, family connections, or personal ability has caused some of them to be well remembered in Charleston to this day: Mary Elizabeth Dulles married Langdon Cheves, speaker of the House of Representatives, Thomas Middleton was a better-than-average artist as well as a prosperous planter, and Thomas Broom served with distinction as an officer on board the U.S.S. Chesapeake in the War of 1812.

Mrs. Cleland Kinloch

Mrs. J. Allen Smith Izard

John S. Cogdell

Mrs. Rawlins Lowndes

Charles Fras

William Robertson

Thomas Middleton

Mrs. Ralph Izard

Mary Theodosia Ford

Henry Broughton Mazyck

Nathaniel Heyward II

John Huger II

Rawlins Lowndes

Mrs. Julius Pringle

Captain Thomas Broom

Mrs. Robert Budd Gilchrist

Mrs. Edward Parker

Mrs. Langdon Cheves

TM
1836

Presbyterian meetinghouse, Prince William's Parish.

Anglican church in St. Andrew's Parish, April, 1800.

58

Dignified worship

in gem-like churches

Charlestonians were a religious people who regarded regular church attendance as both a spiritual and a social obligation. Though Anglicanism was the predominant faith, Nonconformist sects flourished in the city from the beginning. The Huguenots were the first, establishing a congregation in 1680, and services in their church were conducted in French until this century. On Sunday the aristocracy could be observed in churches like St. Michael's or St. Philip's, the latter shown at left in an 1836 painting by Thomas Middleton. In the years after the Revolution, the rector of St. Michael's was Henry Purcell, whose portrait appears above. Unusually hot-blooded for a gentleman of the cloth, he once challenged a fellow priest to a duel. Charleston gentry also carried their faith with them when they went to the Low Country in the fever-free months; four of the tiny but well-proportioned rural churches in which they worshiped are shown below in a group of water colors by Charles Fraser.

Ruins of Sheldon Church, burned by the British in 1780.

St. James' Church in the Goose Creek area, about 1800.

Charleston today: stately relics of a remembered past

Even today, many parts of Charleston still retain an ante-bellum character. Hardly changed in the last hundred years, these monuments of a prosperous past have managed to survive the ravages of time, war, natural disasters, and modern improvements. Fortunately, tradition-minded Charlestonians have made an effort to save and restore lovely old buildings like the ones on Rainbow Row, shown at right. Built late in the eighteenth century, these pastel-colored houses on East Bay once belonged to rich merchants who lived in the upper floors and transacted their business below.

The ballroom of the William Gibbes House is decorated with Sully portraits, damask curtains, Louis XVI furniture.

One of several ante-bellum public buildings still in use is the temple-like City Market.

Charleston's doorways and decorative ironwork are famous. An earthquake bolt secures the door at left.

"I first saw her on October 18, 1878," he wrote, "and loved her as soon as I saw her sweet, fair young face. We spent three years of happiness such as rarely comes to man or woman." So began a memorial to Alice Hathaway Lee of Chestnut Hill, Massachusetts, written by Theodore Roosevelt some time during 1884. She was remembered but rarely mentioned in the 35 years that followed.

October 18, 1878, was a week before Theodore's twentieth birthday, at the start of his junior year at Harvard. A good many years afterward he was to remark to his friend, Henry White, that women interested him very little, but this was not true in his boyhood and youth. The small boy traveling in Europe had noted in his diary that he sorely missed a playmate, Edith Carow. In the spring of 1876, while preparing to enter Harvard, he had attended a neighborhood party where he had enjoyed the company of "Annie Murray, a very nice girl, besides being very pretty, ahem!" And at Harvard he wrote of his pleasure in the company of two young ladies, "especially pretty Alice."

A tendency to lead the conversation into dull paths of natural science may have minimized his appeal to girls at first. Cambridge changed this. His intimates at the Porcellian Club found him, though still overenthusiastic about botany and bugs, entirely acceptable. Their sisters, if amused, liked him. As Theodore's junior year ended he had even become a romantic figure; while his classmates worried about examinations and indulged only in sedate flirtations under a Victorian moon, he was in the throes of a turbulent love affair. It was known that he planned to be married immediately after graduation.

He met Alice Lee that October, at the home of Richard Saltonstall, one of Theodore's closest friends. In November he wrote his sister Conie that with Minot Weld, another intimate, he had driven to Saltonstall's home at Chestnut Hill and had "gone out walking with Miss Rose Saltonstall and Miss Alice Lee." Some weeks later he escorted Alice through the Harvard Yard and, while pointing out the beauties of the institution, discovered that it was time for lunch. He promptly took his guest to the Porcellian Club, never before polluted by the presence of a woman. The assertion that he did this was published while Roosevelt was alive, in a biography written by Jacob Riis and published with his approval. Presumably Roosevelt would have denied the incident had it been untrue. But no mention of it is found in any of his letters, and only conjecture is possible as to Theodore's reason for such radical conduct. It had been his invariable custom to lunch at the Porc house, and it may never

" ...*Especially*

During their courtship exuberant your

Alice Lee, but they had three idyllic yea

By HENI

have occurred to him that he was shattering precedent. He may have already been anesthetized by love. He may have believed the rule against women foolish nonsense, for he had strong feminist leanings in those remote days and his senior dissertation was on "The Practicability of Equalizing Men and Women Before the Law."

She walked the stage for so brief a moment, there are so few who can remember and fewer still who will,

HARVARD UNIVERSITY

pretty Alice."

...heodore Roosevelt puzzled the delicate

...f marriage before tragedy separated them

PRINGLE

At Harvard in 1878 Roosevelt (far left) was a bare-chested, bewhiskered boxer, plucky in the ring but so nearsighted he could barely see his opponent. Courting Alice Lee, he insisted she witness his bid for the college lightweight title; the gently bred Alice was repelled but also intrigued.

that Alice Lee remains a fragment. But only partly. To Theodore she was "beautiful in face and form, and lovelier still in spirit," but she was lovely, too, to those who looked with less prejudiced eyes. It is known that she was seventeen on the October day when they met. Her hair was light brown with, in the sun, a touch of yellow. She wore it in curls that lay well back, over smaller curls which came down over her high forehead. Her nose tilted ever so slightly; her mouth was small and "peculiarly charming." She was about five feet seven inches in height, and this, combined with an erect carriage, made her seem rather tall.

She was the daughter of George C. Lee of Chestnut Hill, and her family tree bore Cabots and Lees and Higginsons on all its branches. When Theodore met her in 1878 she had seen little or nothing of society, and her education had been the ornamentally fashionable one received by young gentlewomen of the day.

It was a turbulent courtship. Mrs. Robert Bacon, then sixteen, long recalled a function of the Hasty Pudding Club at which Roosevelt had walked up, had pointed across the room to Alice, and had demanded:

"See that girl? I am going to marry her. She won't have me, but I am going to have *her!*"

Mrs. Bacon remembered, too, that the gentle Alice was alarmed by the impetuosity of the young man who had suddenly precipitated himself into the circle of more decorous beaux. He had an overwhelming, gusty vitality and he insisted that she watch, from the gymnasium balcony, when he made his bid for the lightweight boxing championship. Alice was a little repelled but wholly intrigued. Besides, there was no way in which she could avoid seeing him had she so desired. Richard Saltonstall, a cousin, was constantly bringing him to the house on week ends. He had a habit of throwing himself into a chair and telling thrilling stories about wolves and bears to her adoring five-year-old brother.

Alice sometimes discouraged the eager Theodore, and then he was plunged into the deepest gloom. He was always to suffer periods of discouragement, when everything seemed black. These were moments of despair. One night, during the first winter of the courtship, a classmate telegraphed to New York in alarm that Roosevelt was somewhere in the woods near Cambridge and refused to come home. A cousin who was particularly close hurried up there, managed somehow to soothe him; and soon his confidence returned.

The courtship continued through the winter and spring of 1878–79, with Theodore becoming markedly possessive as the months passed. During the summer, beyond doubt, he wrote long and fervent letters, for it was his unfailing custom to do so on all subjects at all times, in private life as well as when he held office. That he suffered recurring attacks of jealousy is probable, particularly when Alice sent back accounts of picnics and festivities among the boys and girls of Chestnut Hill.

That he had already told his family about Alice is demonstrated by an invitation extended to the girl and her mother to spend the Christmas holidays at Oyster Bay. Theodore's mother seems to have been fond of Alice from the start; nor is this surprising. The young girl and the older woman had much in common. They were gentle and rather quiet. They had charm and grace. Both, for by now Alice's last defenses had been shattered, considered Theodore wholly magnificent. The brief days between Christmas, 1878, and New Year's Day of 1879 must have been high marks in Theodore's life. He saw Alice, who affected heavy white brocades to set off her fair hair and blue eyes, standing in front of the open fire after dinner; Alice being very feminine, very attentive to the conversation, very timid about taking more than a sip of wine. He saw her, demure in furs and carrying a small muff, while she skated on nearby ponds and leaned deliciously on his strong arms.

Meanwhile, in the Yard, Roosevelt was a marked man. It now became apparent that he was neglecting his editorial duties on the *Advocate* because of more important activities at Chestnut Hill. Rumors of his preoccupation even reached the ears of the cloistered faculty. One morning, in the English and rhetoric class, Professor A. S. Hill, familiarly called "Ass" Hill, read aloud an unusually sentimental essay and cruelly asked Theodore to criticize it. His classmates assumed, from the fact that he blushed, that he was the author. The Dickey show, as far back as the previous year, had commented on his courting as well as on his elegant appearance.

At about this time Roosevelt's interest in the natural sciences began to flag. The evidence is not conclusive. Alice may have expressed distaste for squirrels and birds no longer alive but looking as dead as only an amateur taxidermist could make them look. A fragment of a letter remains, written in July of 1879, in which Theodore told his friend Harry Minot that he had done almost no collecting that summer, that "I don't approve of too much slaughter."

So Alice became his. She was an engaged girl. Her mind turned to the wedding, which had been tentatively set for the following October, and to such pleasant labors as her wedding gown and the countless linens that every young bride of that day considered essential. Theodore, even after the engagement was formally announced, could find no peace. He worried when some classmate, anxious to show polite attention to his fiancée, talked with her at a dance.

"Roosevelt," recalled a member of Alice's family, "seemed constantly afraid that some one would run off with her, and threatened duels and everything else. On one occasion he actually sent abroad for a set of French dueling pistols, and after great difficulty got them through the Custom House."

Theodore's honor was not impugned, however. No blood was shed. He managed to get his degree despite the distractions at Chestnut Hill. He became a Bachelor of Arts, by grace of Harvard College, on June 30, 1880. He took no prominent part in the exercises. Roosevelt did not attempt to begin the pursuit of a career that summer. The estate of his father had made him a young man of means, although not of wealth. There was no need to hurry. Meanwhile, a degree of ill health on the part of his brother Elliott offered excuse for a hunting trip that summer. The trip was a great success despite "a succession of untoward accidents and delays. I got bitten by a snake and chucked head foremost out of the wagon."

Then Roosevelt hurried to Chestnut Hill, and the marriage took place at Brookline on October 27, 1880. The day was Theodore's twenty-second birthday, while Alice was nineteen.

The honeymoon was delayed, apparently, until the next summer, for the young couple went to New York to live with Theodore's widowed mother at No. 6 West Fifty-seventh Street, an address considered uptown and out of the way, but beginning to be fashionable.

Having abandoned science, Theodore had decided to take up law, and this was the reason for postponing the honeymoon. He was not greatly interested in the law, but it was something to do, and so he enrolled at the Columbia Law School and also did some reading in the office of his uncle, Robert Barnhill Roosevelt. The twelve months that followed Roosevelt's marriage constitute a period of uncertainty. He did a little work on his *The Naval War of 1812*, of which a chapter or two had been written at Cambridge. He started to take notice of local politics, also, but here, too, signs of active interest are lacking. He joined the district Republican Club in the fall of 1880 for the reason that "a young man of my bringing up and convictions could join only the Republican Party"; a curious statement, since both his uncle and father-in-law were Democrats. So life drifted, with frequent social affairs in which Alice and his mother were joint hostesses, and with life at home unmarked by the slightest friction between the mother and the daughter-in-law.

A trip to Europe, Theodore's third in less than fifteen years, provided a pleasant diversion during the summer of 1881. With Alice, he was in England in time for spring. They went north into Ireland and set

CONTINUED ON PAGE 103

HENRY FORD
and his
PEACE SHIP

"We're going to try to get the boys out of the trenches before Christmas," the confident auto-maker said. "I've chartered a ship, and some of us are going to Europe." This much-ridiculed attempt to stop the European war in 1916 is given a fresh, impartial evaluation in the second of a definitive series of books on Ford, recently published by Charles Scribner's Sons.

Excerpted from:
Ford: Expansion and Challenge, 1915–1933

By ALLAN NEVINS *and* FRANK ERNEST HILL

Henry Ford's intensive peace activities really began in November, 1915, when a company car drew up at the Ten Eyck house, his temporary home on the Fair Lane estate, bringing two guests. One was Rosika Schwimmer, Hungarian author and lecturer, a dark, stout, vibrant woman in her late thirties who had served such causes as woman suffrage, birth control, and trade unionism. Her companion, Louis P. Lochner, a slender, blond young American, had recently acted as secretary of the International Federation of Students. Both were now workers for world peace.

From the beginning of the war an advocate of mediation by neutrals, Rosika Schwimmer in April, 1915, had helped persuade the International Congress of Women at The Hague to support such a policy. She assisted Jane Addams and others to gather evidence that both neutrals and belligerents were receptive to mediation. When she came to the United States as a lecturer later in the year, she brought documents that allegedly proved the existence of such an attitude. Madame Schwimmer noted Henry Ford's declaration in August, 1915, that he was prepared to dedicate his fortune and his life to achieving peace, wrote to him, and through Edwin G. Pipp of the Detroit *News* eventually procured an interview. She aroused Ford's interest, and after seeing her documents he remarked: "Well, let's start. What do you want me to do?"

Lochner arrived in Detroit at this time, also seeking an interview with Ford. He came fresh from a conference which he and David Starr Jordan, president of Stanford University and chairman of the Fifth International Peace Congress, had held in Washington with President Woodrow Wilson. Lochner felt that if a greater popular demand for peace could be demonstrated, Wilson might call a conference at Washington, where representatives of neutral nations would appoint a commission to work unremittingly ("continuous mediation") for a peace acceptable to all belligerents.

After the two had arrived at the Ten Eyck house, Ford left Madame Schwimmer with his wife, Clara, "to talk things over," and hustled Lochner off to his experimental tractor shop. There he took him aside and demanded: "What do you think of Madame Schwimmer's proposal? Is it practical? How much will it cost to maintain a neutral commission in Europe?"

Lochner warmly supported the idea of continuous mediation, and also suggested that Ford seek an interview with President Wilson at which he could offer to maintain an official commission abroad until Congress made an appropriation; this failing, he could support an unofficial body which would perform comparable work. Ford listened closely and seemed to approve. When they returned to the Ten Eyck house, they found that Clara Ford had been won over to the cause of "continuous mediation." Appealing to her as a mother, Madame Schwimmer had proposed that she finance a barrage of telegrams to the White House supporting that policy. These would fortify a personal plea which Schwimmer and Mrs. Philip Snowden of England were to make to Wilson on November 26. Ford approved the estimated expenditure of $10,000. Then Madame Schwimmer left for New York, Ford

At the rail of the Oscar II *just before departure Henry Ford vainly offers Thomas Edison $1,000,000 to sail with the peace mission. The party includes* (from left): *S. S. McClure, magazine publisher and editor of the New York* Evening Mail; *Louis P. Lochner, who suggested the idea of a peace ship to Ford and became his chief lieutenant; the ship's captain; Ford; Edison; Rosika Schwimmer, Hungarian writer and lecturer who was also one of the expedition's organizers; Judge Ben Lindsey of Denver; and the Reverend Jenkin Lloyd Jones, midwestern editor, pacifist, and Unitarian minister.*

Gorsline

and Lochner agreeing to follow the next afternoon.

As the two men were borne eastward the following day, Ford was as happy as if he had hatched an idea for a revolutionary new motor car. He bubbled with talk. Lochner noted his keen instinct for publicity. "Whatever we decide to do," declared the manufacturer, "New York is the place for starting it." He revealed a gift for epigram, striking off such crisp pronouncements as: "Men sitting around a table, not men dying in a trench, will finally settle the differences." He watched Lochner closely and, if he detected a favorable response, would say: "Make a note of that; we'll give that to the boys when we get to New York."

He established himself at the Biltmore Hotel and on the following day, November 21, lunched with a group at the McAlpin. It included Jane Addams of Hull House, Chicago; Dean George W. Kirchwey of Columbia University; Paul Kellogg of the *Survey;* and, of course, Lochner and Madame Schwimmer. All approved the plan of sending if possible an official mediating commission to Europe; failing that, a representative private group. Ford and Lochner would go to Washington to seek Wilson's co-operation, which would invest the project with an official status.

In the talk at table, Lochner half jestingly suggested: "Why not a special ship to take the delegates over?" Ford's approval flashed like a light to the click of a switch. In vain Jane Addams objected to the plan as flamboyant; Ford liked it for that very reason. Men could see it; it would lift talk into action and arouse a sharper interest. He sent at once for representatives of

steamship companies and, posing as "Mr. Henry," inquired what it would cost to charter a vessel. The agents stared at him, but when told his identity quickly made their calculations. Having started negotiations, Ford waved them over to Rosika Schwimmer, and by evening she had chartered the Scandinavian-American liner *Oscar II.*

Through Colonel Edward M. House, then in New York, Ford procured an appointment with President Wilson for the following day. Promising a group of reporters that he would see them Wednesday, he and Lochner left for Washington.

The conference with the President began pleasantly. "Mr. Ford slipped unceremoniously into an armchair, and during most of the interview had his left leg hanging over the arm of the chair and swinging back and forth," Lochner observed.

Ford complimented the President on his appearance; how did he keep so trim? Wilson replied that he tried to forget business after business hours and to enjoy a good joke. "Some of them Ford jokes, I hope?" suggested Lochner. Ford then told one such story he had invented himself.

One day, he said, driving by a cemetery, he had noticed a huge hole being dug by a gravedigger and asked him if he were going to bury a whole family in one grave. The man replied No, that the grave was for one person. Then why was it so enormous? The gravedigger explained that the deceased was a queer fellow and had stipulated in his will that he must be buried in his Ford, because the Ford had pulled him out of every hole thus far, and he was sure it would pull him out of this one.

Wilson chuckled and capped it with a limerick. Then Ford explained his mission. He urged Wilson to appoint a neutral commission, offering to finance it. The President replied that he did not feel able to take such a step. He approved the idea of continuing mediation, but a better plan might be offered. He

William Jennings Bryan, who approved of the mission but did not accompany it, waves good-by from the dock.

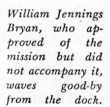

Gorsline

could not be tied to any one project; he must be free.

This was too equivocal for Ford. He said that he had chartered a steamship and had promised the press an announcement on the following morning. He offered the ship to the President. "If you feel you can't act, I will." Wilson was startled but stood by his first statement, and Ford and Lochner soon found themselves on the White House grounds. Ford shook his head, but if his companion feared for the fate of the expedition, he was quickly reassured. Ford was only regretful that the President had missed a great opportunity. "He's a small man," he said.

Even before the appointed hour of ten on Wednesday the twenty-fourth, reporters began to arrive at the Biltmore. With Lochner and Oswald Garrison Villard, whom he had expressly asked to be present (the New York *Times* reported Jane Addams and Ida M. Tarbell also there), Ford chatted with the newsmen until forty had gathered, a number which somewhat abashed him. He began rather haltingly: "A man should always try to do the greatest good to the greatest number, shouldn't he?" He went on: "We're going to try to get the boys out of the trenches before Christmas. I've chartered a ship, and some of us are going to Europe."

Lochner and Villard supplied details. Asked about the ship and its voyage, Ford stated that he would assemble a group "of the biggest and most influential peace advocates in the country, who can get away, on this ship." He would also have "the longest gun in the world—the Marconi." Jane Addams, John Wanamaker, and Thomas A. Edison would sail with him.

The interview was page one news for New York papers and, in consequence, for most others. But from the beginning a vein of satire was apparent:

GREAT WAR ENDS
CHRISTMAS DAY
FORD TO STOP IT

announced the *Tribune*. The *World, Times,* and *Evening Post* were more factual. Only a flicker of humor lit the news accounts. For two days there were no editorials.

When they came, satire was more pronounced, often veering toward invective. American opinion, molded by the *Lusitania* and other submarine sinkings and by skilled Allied propaganda, was increasingly anti-German. Also, men tended to believe that only a clear Allied victory could insure a satisfactory peace.

The general chorus was condemnatory. The *World*, usually friendly to Ford, called the peace ship an "impossible effort to establish an inopportune peace." The New York *Herald* termed it "one of the cruellest jokes of the century." The Hartford *Courant* remarked that

"Henry Ford's latest performance is getting abundant criticism and seems entitled to all it gets."

Along with such cutting comment by editors ran a *leitmotiv* of raillery in news reports, letters, and verse. John O'Keefe dashed off "The Flivvership," which the *World* printed on the same day and page as its editorial. One verse ran:

> *I saw a little fordship*
> *Go chugging out to sea,*
> *   And for a flag*
> *   It bore a tag*
> *   Marked 70 h.p.*
> *And all the folk aboardship*
> *Cried "Hail to Hennery!"*

It is only just to note certain factors bearing on the peace ship which were ignored by most commentators at the time and have never been given the attention they deserve. Particularly should Ford's pacifism and his project be considered in relation to the peace movement of his day.

While his aversion to war flared out intensely in 1915, we have no direct evidence as to how it had developed. A year later one writer asserted that it had been implanted from childhood by his mother, Mary Litogot Ford. Her personal experiences in the Civil War, including her son's birth during it, were represented as so affecting her that "she gave to Henry Ford an inherited aversion to war."

This statement is more than plausible. It is also possible that both Mary Ford and her son were influenced by Mary's adopted father, Patrick O'Hern, who deserted from the British Army in Canada and presumably had no love for things military. Furthermore, an aversion to war may have marked the Ford side of the family. Of a dozen Fords of military age in the Dearborn area in 1861, including Henry's father, William, not one volunteered to serve the Union.

Actually, Ford grew up in an era marked by an increasing devotion to peace. When he was beginning his experiments with the automobile in the 1890's the few faltering peace societies of the early nineteenth century had become many, strong, and influential. The cause of international arbitration, receiving its first great impetus from the successful work of the Geneva Tribunal in settling Anglo-American differences in 1871, and supported by Quakers, Manchester Liberals, and international business interests, had enlisted many authors and editors. When in 1899 Czar Nicholas II called a conference at The Hague to codify the laws of war and establish a Court of International Arbitration, the event seemed to confirm the value of their work, as did a second conference in 1904.

Even before the first Hague conference Alfred

Nobel of Sweden had established a Peace Prize of 150,000 kroner for "the man or woman who, during the year, has contributed most . . . to the cause of peace." Ideas of the humanization and prevention of war continued to grow. A brilliant Englishman, Norman Angell, attacked motivations for war in *The Great Illusion* (1908), arguing that the victor as well as the vanquished lost by it. In the United States the American School Peace League (1907) fostered peace sentiment in the public schools, peace societies multiplied, and peace magazines flourished. Theodore Roosevelt had won the Nobel Peace Prize in 1904 for helping to end the Russo-Japanese War, and two institutions had been founded in 1910 to combat war: Edwin Ginn's World Peace Foundation and Andrew Carnegie's Endowment for International Peace.

Pacifism in the United States on the eve of World War I was thus not only respectable but little short of triumphant. An atmosphere of faith in the goodness of mankind hung over the country like a spell of golden weather. The Hague conferences, the adjudication of fourteen disputes by the International Court of Arbitration, the signing of arbitration treaties—such events seemed milestones leading to a glorious goal. Young intellectuals earnestly discussed the probable span of time—ten, twenty-five, or fifty years—before war would become extinct.

These talks did not live by the ideal of peace alone. New winds of thought and aspiration from other sources were then blowing across the United States and the world. The ideas of Theodore Roosevelt on social justice and Woodrow Wilson's New Freedom fortified all believers in a nobler world. Henry Ford had not read Upton Sinclair's *The Jungle*, Jack London's *The People of the Abyss*, or John Spargo's *The Bitter Cry of the Children*, but he knew that the protest against human exploitation was gaining volume. He knew something of what Tom L. Johnson of Cleveland, Ben Lindsey of Denver, and Jane Addams stood for, and he moved among men and women who carried the dream of a more just, serene, and joyful world through their hours of work and leisure. Great hopes were in the air; a new age was being born when the war of 1914 lurched across it like an artillery caisson over a bed of flowers.

If the war shattered the mood of the time, it also aroused fierce resentment and intensified bruised hopes. Pacifists proclaimed the conflict to be merely a frightful demonstration of the rightness of all they had said. Peace societies were more aggressive than ever. In verse and prose American writers lifted voices of protest. An immense section of the public was receptive toward any step likely to hasten the end of the slaughter. Ford himself, who had hitherto been silent but

like others had now stepped forth to testify, spoke in the spirit of the time. His was no wild, perverse crusade; he was marching along the same road that Hay, Root, Taft, Bryan, and others had traveled, and millions in spirit marched with him.

He had already won an important objective: he had aroused the widest possible attention. Could the venture, even if born in ridicule, be so managed as to impress the watching world? One element was time: time for effective organization, time for eminent individuals to adjust their affairs to the voyage. It would have been wiser to postpone a public announcement until a number of distinguished guests had been pledged. But the announcement having been made when it was, Ford could still have associated the project with the new year rather than with Christmas, gaining a month or more. He and his associates could then have planned the cruise more carefully, enhanced the chances of success, and safeguarded the dignity of the enterprise. Instead, announcing December 4 as the date of sailing, he left only nine days for assembling guests and planning the expedition. This was stacking the cards against his project from the start.

Why did Ford set himself this all but insuperable challenge? The answer lay in his own character. He had never followed conventional paths and delighted in the seemingly impossible. Doubtless he felt that he and his associates could rise to the emergency, and that the sensation would be the greater. Again, he craved action. For half a year he had been writing and talking against preparedness and war and had built up a reservoir of explosive energy. Moreover, something could be said for speed. It might accomplish more than a deliberate procedure with its delayed impact. As to the dignity of the expedition, had anyone mentioned it, Ford would have responded with a snort.

At Ford's suite in the Biltmore, headquarters for the enterprise, Gaston Plantiff, manager of the New York branch of the Ford company, began to plan the administration of the cruise and soon staffed it with dozens of workers. Ford and Rosika Schwimmer began to send out invitations.

Characteristically, Ford himself did not help organize the crusade. Schwimmer and Lochner were at hand. Schwimmer regarded the crusade as a project of her own to which Ford had attached himself, and she was eager to manage it. Tacitly he let her do this (apart from matters in Plantiff's hands), shunting Lochner into the post of her general assistant. In leaving chief authority to Madame Schwimmer, Ford made a serious error. She was an enemy alien, a fact which many Americans and other neutrals never forgot. Intelligent enough to perceive the delicacy of her status, she made a pretense of keeping in the background. This proved impracticable because of her striking appearance and aggressive manner.

Work began at once with the invitations to prospective guests. Within a day of Ford's first announcement both Edison and John Wanamaker denied that they would go. Jane Addams, however, still planned to sail. Ford appealed to John Burroughs, Luther Burbank, William Howard Taft, Bryan, David Starr Jordan, and other distinguished Americans. The full list numbered 115.

The work was scarcely begun when Schwimmer, Ford, and Lochner went to Washington for the interview which Mrs. Philip Snowden and Schwimmer had obtained with Wilson on November 26. At a preliminary mass meeting in the Belasco Theatre, Ford sat on the platform while the two women addressed the audience. Finally there were calls: "We want Ford!" He was terrified and whispered to Lochner, "You say it for me." Lochner urged: "Just say a few words!" At length Ford rose, cried, "Out of the trenches by Christmas, never to return!" and darted off the stage as if the applause were a pursuing monster.

Ford left that evening for Detroit. Despite his absence, despite haste and confusion, the expedition gained recruits. Within three days thirteen guests had accepted, among them the Reverend Jenkin Lloyd Jones, widely known throughout the Middle West, and the Reverend Charles F. Aked of San Francisco, formerly pastor of John D. Rockefeller's Fifth Avenue Baptist Church in New York. Various eminent individuals and minority groups approved the venture, but many American leaders attacked it. Alton B. Parker, Democratic candidate for President in 1904, called Ford "a clown strutting on the stage for a little time," and Theodore Roosevelt, remarking that he rarely found himself agreeing with Parker, declared that "Mr. Ford's visit abroad will not be mischievous only because it is ridiculous." President John Grier Hibben of Princeton University refused to send a student; Dr. Charles W. Eliot of Harvard said that the mission must fail because it was wrong. The Detroit *Saturday Night* proclaimed Ford's voyage "a humiliation to his city and his country."

Refusals from distinguished men and women poured in: William Dean Howells, Colonel E. M. House, Cardinal Gibbons, William Howard Taft, Louis Brandeis, Morris Hillquit, and others. However, many in declining sent heartening messages. "I cannot too highly commend you," telegraphed Governor Hiram Johnson from California; Ida M. Tarbell disagreed only with the means of seeking peace, not the end. The poet Vachel Lindsay wired: "I am in full sympathy with your expedition." Luther Burbank declared: "My heart is

with you," and Helen Keller, declining because of speaking engagements, announced that she was with Ford "heart and soul." Acceptances grew: S. S. McClure, noted magazine publisher, at this time editor of the New York *Evening Mail;* Governor Louis B. Hanna of North Dakota; Inez Milholland Boissevain, Junoesque beauty and feminist. Elmer Davis, then little known, was among the reporters.

On December 1 came word that Jane Addams, suddenly taken ill, could not make the voyage. She might have to undergo an operation. "It is even doubtful if she can follow later," reported her associate Dr. Alice Hamilton. The loss to the expedition was a bitter one, for Miss Addams might have contributed a stability which the leadership of the crusade sadly lacked.

For a time it seemed that William Jennings Bryan would become a delegate. He arrived in New York on December 2, just after Ford returned from Detroit with Marquis, Clara Ford, and Edsel. The two were already acquainted; earlier in the year Bryan, then secretary of state, had sent Ford a paperweight made from the steel of plowshares. (He had presented such souvenirs to foreign diplomats on the signing of arbitration treaties.) Bryan waited patiently for five hours to see Ford, the two men all but embraced, and Bryan gave out a statement approving the expedition and proposing to join it at The Hague.

Despite the loss of Bryan and Miss Addams, by the eve of sailing the group of delegates was as large and distinguished as Ford and his associates had a right to expect on nine days' notice. No first-rank American leaders like Taft, Edison, or Bryan had joined the party, but McClure, Aked, Judge Ben Lindsey of Denver, and others were nationally known. That so large a group, many of intelligence and reputation, would leave their work for a long trip on scant notice, often making financial sacrifices, was a tribute both to Ford and to the appeal of the undertaking.

Meanwhile, in Detroit a determined effort had been made by Dean Marquis and Clara Ford to dissuade the manufacturer from boarding the *Oscar II*. Marquis from the start had distrusted Schwimmer and Lochner; as refusals multiplied he was convinced that the peace ship delegates would not properly represent America. Mrs. Ford opposed the voyage on more personal grounds. She made Marquis promise that if, despite their efforts, Ford insisted on going, he would accompany and protect him. Failing in Detroit, they came to New York still hopeful, and "sat up all night" with Ford on the eve of the voyage, expostulating, arguing, cajoling. With Marquis' resourceful eloquence and Clara's tears, it was a powerful attack. The very fate of the voyage hung in the balance, for without Ford the ship would have lacked its most powerful symbol and moral force. But he withstood the assault.

The day of sailing was as busy as any preceding it. At the Biltmore, Ford faced a group of reporters. Had he a last word for the public?

"Yes. Tell the people to cry peace and fight preparedness."

"What if the expedition fails?"

"I'll start another."

As he left the hotel in a Model T touring car for Hoboken, where the *Oscar II* rode, with Clara, Edsel, and the sculptor C. S. Pietro, he announced: "We've got peace-talk going now, and I'll pound it to the end."

At the Hoboken dock, despite a raw, cold day, a crowd estimated at 15,000 had gathered for the sail-

"The Tug of Peace"

ing. People filled the pier, with more constantly arriving. The Fords appeared, greeted by resounding cheers. Soon afterward, Bryan approached the ship. The band struck up "I Didn't Raise My Boy to Be a Soldier," the crowd roared, and the commoner made "many sweeping bows" as he went smiling up the gangplank. On board, he acted as a witness at the marriage of the poet Berton Braley and Miss Marian Rubicam. The reporters reveled in the episode as fully in the spirit of the cruise and were almost as enthusiastic about two caged squirrels, dispatched to Ford on the ship by some prankster to live happily among the "nuts." (One was later christened "William Jennings Bryan" and the other "Henry Ford" by the reporters.)

The Fords chatted with the Edisons and other friends. According to William C. Bullitt of the Philadelphia *Ledger,* Ford urged Edison: "You must stay on board, you must stay on board." Then, with a quizzical smile but (thought Bullitt) "intense seriousness," he said: "I'll give you a million dollars if you'll come." Because of his deafness Edison couldn't hear; Ford repeated the offer but the inventor smiled and shook his head. However, he assured his friend that he was heart and soul with him. Later Edison and his wife left with Edsel and Clara Ford, down whose cheeks tears were streaming. Dean Marquis, as he had promised Mrs. Ford, had taken passage with her husband. The Fords and Edisons stood on the pier until the ship left.

As it did so, in a final touch of the mad circus atmosphere of the occasion, a figure leaped from the pier and swam stoutly after it. Rescued, he announced himself as "Mr. Zero" and explained that he was "swimming to reach public opinion." Meanwhile the crowd, oblivious to most of these decorative incidents, warmed to the departure. It stood waving and roaring: it "cheered and yelled until it had no voice left." According to Lochner, Ford was exalted. "Again and again he bowed, his face wreathed in smiles that gave it a beatific expression. The magnitude of the demonstration—many a strong man there was who struggled in vain against tears born of deep emotion —quite astonished and overwhelmed him. I felt then that he considered himself amply repaid for all the ridicule heaped upon him."

As the *Oscar II* slipped out of New York harbor in the fading light and pointed her nose northeast, she was perhaps the first physical missile ever launched against a war. Nobody was sure what effect she would have. Dozens of reporters described the vessel's progress in day-to-day stories; later it provoked magazine articles, chapters in books, and at least one complete volume. Significantly, its ideological character dominated all these accounts. It was not a ship, but *the* peace ship. Actual details about vessel and mission are hard to come by, for it was the pilgrims and their quest that fascinated every observer.

The group was a strange one—not, as Mary Alden Hopkins tried to persuade herself, "representative: a cross-section of America." Almost half the delegates were writers (many suffragists, socialists, single-taxers, or pacifists); the next largest segment comprised lecturers and workers for causes; there were a few government officials, ministers, teachers. No business men, farmers, industrialists (except Ford), scientists, engineers, or labor officials were included. While a few delegates like S. S. McClure and Governor Hanna were "practical," the great majority were social evangelists of some kind. The reporters, who never gave the finer personalities the respect they deserved, probably pronounced the careless American's appraisal in terming the shipload "a bunch of nuts."

Naturally, the center of interest for both delegates and journalists was Henry Ford, for all hoped that on shipboard he could be studied at leisure. Ford was cooperative. When a wave drenched him one morning as he was briskly walking the deck and he caught cold, he was of course no longer available. But the reporters, skeptical at first, by that time had been converted. Ford's complete sincerity, his friendliness, his pithy, quotable comments, won them all. Bullitt says they were convinced that the manufacturer was "an absolutely unselfish egoist." "Ford is really Christlike," Bullitt recorded. He liked the realism with which Ford appraised the voyage.

"Don't you feel that this is a holy cause?" a minister asked him.

"No," Ford replied. "I don't know what you mean by holy. Instead of a holy cause I consider this expedition a people's affair."

"Are you not sailing with faith?" persisted the other.

"Yes," agreed Ford, "but it is faith in the people. I have absolute confidence in the better side of human nature . . . People never disappoint you if you trust them. Only three out of six hundred convicts in my factory have failed to make good."

Ford stated frankly what he expected from the expedition. It was not to bring peace immediately, but to hasten it. "The chief effect I look for is psychological." The peace ship was an advertisement for peace. "I consider that the peace ship will have been worth while if it does nothing more than it has done already in driving preparedness off the front page of the newspapers and putting peace on the front page."

On the third night out Ford sent an exhortation to members of Congress by wireless, urging them "to give the peace mission your support and encouragement so that it may succeed at the earliest possible moment." The following day he radioed messages to a number of

rulers, pleading for peace. "Enough blood has been shed, enough agony endured, enough destruction wrought." He begged them to declare a truce and by "mediation and discussion" to settle what was not being settled by the guns. These bulletins made good copy for the reporters. Ford had unlimbered his "longest gun in the world," and the peace ship seemed not altogether futile.

On December 9 occurred the most sensational event of the voyage. Two nights before, McClure had read President Wilson's message to Congress. It was a plea for preparedness, advocating an increase in the standing army. A committee of delegates had been appointed to draft resolutions on the message, to be signed and sent to Congress. On the ninth, after Lochner had made a plea for immediate disarmament, Dr. Aked rose and read the Declaration of Principles of the Ford Peace Party, the work of the committee. Deprecating military preparedness, it pledged all delegates to work for international disarmament. The declaration was to be left four or five days for "examination and signing," the assumption being that all delegates would sign. But a number, although eager to see the war ended, did not favor critical comment upon their President or Congress. Said McClure:

"For years I have been working for international disarmament. I have visited the capitals of Europe time and time again in its behalf. But I cannot impugn the course laid out by the President of the United States and supported by my newspaper. I should like to be able to go on working with the party, but I am unable to sign that part of its declaration of principles which would place me in opposition to my Government."

Judge Lindsey took essentially the same stand, with Governor Hanna, the journalist John D. Barry, Herman Bernstein, and others. Madame Schwimmer and Jenkin Lloyd Jones, according to Bullitt, accused McClure of corrupting the students of the party by talking preparedness to them, while Lochner exclaimed: "Any one who accepted the invitation of Mr. Ford, and now refuses to sign this resolution, came for a free ride!" This comment was resented. Barry protested bitterly: "If you push through this resolution and cause a sharp split in the party, we shall be the laughing-stock of the whole of Europe."

The conflict should have been foreseen before the voyage began. Ford, it is true, was as fervidly against preparedness as war. But the success of the expedition was his objective. To win it he was seeking the co-operation of all neutral nations and was heartened by Madame Schwimmer's documents indicating that even the belligerents were receptive to peace talks. He was pledged to seek *their* aid. How then could he logically object to peace-lovers who believed in a measure of preparedness? But the policy of the expedition had never been thought through, and such extremists as Jones, Schwimmer, Lochner, and Aked stood ready to demand that everyone approve the declaration or leave the party at the first possible port. "Pacifist," remarked Bullitt, "means a person hard to pacify."

In the end, a statement signed by Ford, while stressing the point that to work for peace and even tacitly condone preparedness was impossible (a wholly illogical assertion, of course), emphasized that all delegates were welcome in the crusade. But the reporters joyfully advertised the rift in the party. "The dove of peace has taken flight," cried the Chicago *Tribune*, "chased off by the screaming eagle." The press throughout the world carried accounts of the quarrel. "Thank heaven," newsmen were quoted as saying, "at last a story has broken!" Later the journalists were accused of having magnified the dispute. "The amount of wrangling has been picturesquely exaggerated," wrote Mary Alden Hopkins on her return to New York. "A man does not become a saint by stepping on a peace boat."

With more justification, the delegates resented the persistent levity and ridicule which marked many reporters' dispatches, and the downright falsehoods occasionally perpetrated. "The expedition has been hampered at every step by the direct and indirect influence of the American press, by the Atlantic seaboard press,"

declared one of the party who returned to write about it while its work was still going forward. Lochner in his book fully agreed. He tells how Captain J. W. Hempel of the *Oscar II,* who read everything sent out by wireless from his ship, brought some of the more obnoxious dispatches to Ford, asking if they should be sent. Ford replied, "Let them send anything they please. They are my guests. I wouldn't for the world censor them." Later he insisted: "Our work will speak for itself." Some reporters repaid this courtesy by forcing their way into Ford's stateroom during his illness to see if he were actually alive!

The ship approached the British Isles by the northern route above Scotland on its way to Norway. As Ford, exhausted and suffering from his cold, kept to his cabin, the position of Madame Schwimmer became somewhat clearer to the correspondents, but also a matter for suspicion. Was she tampering with their dispatches? What was in her little black bag? Schwimmer finally agreed to show them, then became angry at some disparaging comment, and called the exhibit off. Again, she accepted an invitation to tea, only to become incensed at some new report and to send word that she refused to meet with persons who had insulted her. The journalists remonstrated: they had done nothing of the sort, wanted to be friends, and she should come. She did, to be greeted by hearty applause as she entered the room. "Don't be hypocritical!" she snapped, effectively quashing any good will. She completed the job by accusing the reporters of telling Ford that she listened at keyholes!

The delegates looked forward to their landing in Norway, where Schwimmer promised them a rousing reception. Doubtless many, like Mary Alden Hopkins, were stirred by soaring hopes:

"One hundred and fifty everyday people have been brought face to face with a great idea—the thought of world disarmament. There's no escaping it, short of jumping into the sea. The idea pervades the ship. Groups talk of it. . . . Reporters are nervous lest there's no news value in it. . . . At times the vision comes to all of us—mystic, veiled, and wonderful. Then common sense revolts. Yet we dare not treat the vision with contempt. A ship of fools crossed the Atlantic in 1492. A ship of fools reached Plymouth in 1620. Can it be that in this ship of common fools, we bear the Holy Grail to the helping of a wounded world?"

Norway appeared, rocky, snowbound, forested. As they ran along the coast the delegates stood on the deck, and "for a while there was sublime peace, even on the peace ship." Now the time had passed for aspirations alone; henceforth salvation must be won by works as well as by faith.

It was 4 A.M. on December 18, with the temperature twelve degrees below zero, when the ship docked at Oslo. Later that morning a few Norwegians appeared to welcome the expedition, but there was no reception such as Schwimmer had promised. After breakfast, the delegates took an electric train to a city park, where they enjoyed several hours of sun, fresh air, and crisp snow—their first touch of earth for two weeks. That afternoon they attended a reception by the Women's International Peace League, and in the evening a meeting at the University of Christiania.

The crowd had gathered partly to see Henry Ford and was disappointed; for he, after insisting on walking from the boat to his hotel, had collapsed and gone to bed. He was never to appear in public while in

Life, DECEMBER 30, 1915

"We don't know where we're going, but we're on the way"

Norway. According to Bullitt, the meeting was unsuccessful in other respects. Jenkin Lloyd Jones, after beginning with a pretentious "Hail, Nor-rrway! Hail, Nor-rrway!" bored the intelligent audience with platitudes, and ensuing speakers showed a similar tendency. Fortunately Lochner, clearly outlining the proposed activities of the pilgrims, pleased the Norwegians.

On December 20 the five newspapers of the capital indicated the attitude of the public. Two favored the expedition, and three frowned upon it (one was later to become friendly). The *Tidens Tegn*, the most influential, ridiculed the party but praised Ford. "He is a Tolstoi in a modern edition. He has a personality

which we shall remember long after the expedition is forgotten." Unquestionably one unhappy influence upon the Norwegians was the leadership of Rosika Schwimmer. The Norse thought it wholly unfitting for a citizen of a belligerent power to direct the peace mission of a neutral country. Finally, the Norwegians were in general pro-Ally and felt that a just peace could be concluded only after the German military position had worsened.

Ford had made no progress in overcoming his illness. The weather had been cold and the rooms he occupied faced north. According to Lochner, they could be entered only through those of Dean Marquis or Ray Dahlinger. "Mr. Ford was practically incommunicado." Lochner believed that Marquis, originally opposed to the cruise, had worked steadily on Ford to abandon it and was supported by other Ford employees, both on shipboard and in Detroit. In his weakened state, the manufacturer was of course susceptible to suggestion. Lochner saw the drift of his feeling when he remarked: "Guess I had better go home to mother . . . You've got this thing started now and can get along without me." Lochner protested that Ford's presence was imperative. Besides, should he leave at the first stop in Europe, his act would be interpreted as an admission of failure. Why not go to Finse, a Norwegian health resort, recover there, and rejoin the party later?

Ford agreed to consider this possibility, but his decision had probably been made. If we can trust his statements then and later, he never regretted having launched the expedition. But he probably recognized that it had been badly managed, and that riding herd on the fantastic individualists who composed the party was a difficult task. He was as lost among them as Schwimmer would have been on the assembly line at Highland Park. However, his physical condition seems to have been the determining factor.

At any rate, under Marquis' urging, Ford decided to leave on the morning of December 23 for Bergen, where he could catch the *Bergensfjord*, just sailing for America. As it happened, the delegates were departing a little later that morning for Sweden. Marquis wanted no trouble about Ford's departure. He "spirited" his charge out of the hotel, with a "flying wedge" to make sure that there would be no interference. Lochner and others became aware that something was happening and rushed down to find Ford getting into a taxi. They attempted to question him, but Marquis and his group interposed; there were "a lot of fists flying." Ford and Marquis slipped away in the cab, drove around the delegates' train to their own, and got away as few realized what had happened.

When Ford's flight became generally known, the

effect was much what Lochner had feared. The party felt depressed—even betrayed. Plantiff indicated that Ford would return. "Before leaving, he expressed to me his absolute faith in the party and . . . the earnest hope that all would continue to co-operate to the closest degree in bringing about the desired results which had been so close to his heart—the accomplishment of universal peace."

While this statement reassured the delegates and checked malicious comment, it did not soften the staggering blow of the departure. Of all the party, Ford alone had been of sufficient stature to impress and hearten neutrals. The Christiania *Aftenposten* of December 20 had praised him but lifted its eyebrows at his companions. Bullitt said bluntly that "so far as making an impression on Europe was concerned, the personality of Henry Ford was the party's chief asset." Lochner felt that his going left "a void." Ford's absence also affected the day-to-day conduct of the expedition. While he was with it, there was never any trouble about financing. Furthermore, while he was not pre-eminently an executive, his judgment in emergencies was usually sound. But with the ocean between him and the party, financing became precarious, disagreements began to divide those in charge, and uncertainty developed as to Ford's own wishes. In short, his withdrawal impaired both the prestige and the management of the project.

On returning to New York, apparently with restored health, he denied emphatically that he had "deserted." Illness had hastened his return, but he had never intended to remain long abroad—in fact, had promised his wife to be back "in about five weeks." (He had been gone a month.) He asserted: "I don't regret a single thing I have done. . . . I believe the sentiment we have aroused by making the people think will shorten the war." And when a *Tribune* reporter asked him if he thought the peace ship worth what he had put into it, Ford replied, "I do." Was the kind of publicity he had received satisfactory? "It suited me all right," replied Ford with greater shrewdness than the reporter suspected. "I was bothered only because my wife didn't like some of the criticism. My son, Edsel, didn't mind, and I am really strong for it." He hoped the criticism would continue. Why? "Well," drawled the industrialist, "the best fertilizer in the world is weeds."

In Europe, the expedition had done well. Following Ford's instructions, a committee had been set up "for the management of the trip and policies." It consisted of Jones, Aked, Huebsch, Frederick Holt (Ford's representative), Judge Lindsey, Mrs. Lloyd, Mrs. Fels, and Plantiff, with Lochner as secretary. For a time it worked effectively. What was better, the reception in Sweden was as cordial as that in Norway had been cool. Despite the fact that Christmas holidays were under way, with shops closed and other activities suspended, the residents of Stockholm saw that the pilgrims were well-quartered, organized meetings on their behalf, and showed a warm sympathy with their purpose. But Sweden's fear of Russia made her favorable to a strong Germany and to a peace that would penalize none of the chief combatants.

Denmark was cordial, but unofficially. A recent law forbade addresses by foreigners on the war, and only at "private" meetings of clubs or societies could the delegates present their case. Meanwhile, the problem of getting to Holland loomed up as formidable. A journey by water meant the hazard of mines, while land access was possible only through German territory. Finally, by the unofficial action of the American minister to Denmark, the Germans permitted the entire party to cross their country in a sealed train, and the greater part of the group thus arrived at The Hague. (Aked and Hanna were ill, Canadian-born Julia Wales and the Finnish Mrs. Malmberg were left behind as citizens of belligerent countries; McClure had quitted the expedition.) The Dutch were not wholly enthusiastic about the party, for they had a peace society of their own which had worked along less sensational lines and plainly felt that Ford and his associates were muddying the waters.

After the first golden days in Stockholm, the party had manifested its old disunity. When the personnel of the administrative committee had been announced, Inez Milholland Boissevain had wrathfully protested against undemocratic procedures, and withdrew. Plantiff felt that she was piqued at not having been put on the committee. He had his difficulties running the business end of the enterprise, and was worried about the bickering. He concluded that Schwimmer, who ignored the committee and assumed full authority when it pleased her, was "a woman of a strange and suspicious personality." Some delegates supported her, but she was antagonizing a growing number—particularly Aked, Mrs. Fels, and Barry. "Her presence prejudices every city, her spirit and methods stir up bad blood," Aked was soon to write. The Dutch took the trouble to protest directly to Henry Ford against her.

Having brought the pilgrims through the three Scandinavian countries to Holland, the full circuit of accessible neutral territory, those in charge had now only to choose five delegates to represent the United States on the Neutral Conference for Continuous Mediation and select the site for conference meetings. Jane Addams and William Jennings Bryan were supposedly willing to act as delegates, and there was no question of their being chosen, along with Henry Ford. Plantiff had already arranged with Aked to serve. Mrs. Fels made the fifth representative. As alternates Judge Lindsey, Jenkin Lloyd Jones, Dr. George W. Kirchwey, Emily Greene Balch, and John D. Barry were designated. Of these Americans only Aked from the regular group and Miss Balch from the alternates served for any extended period. Stockholm was selected as the seat of the conference.

The peace party had now completed its task. Plantiff arranged that the students should return to the United States on the *Noordam* (January 11, 1916), the delegates on the *Rotterdam* (January 15). Both groups came back with a variety of attitudes, all praising the purpose of the expedition, but many deploring mistakes in management. The gist of their comment was expressed by (state) Senator Helen Ring Robinson of Denver: "The leaders did not measure up to the bigness of the idea." The reporters took a more satirical view. "The comedy of errors is over," proclaimed T. N. Pockman of the *Tribune*. "During its two months' run the show has aroused more lively interest, cynical amusement and sheer pity than possibly any other in history."

Oddly enough, the return of the pilgrims seemed to be accepted generally as the collapse of Ford's project, although actually it marked the beginning of the real work. This was the task of continuous mediation. One delegate, Florence L. Lattimore, pointed out this fact, adding that "if you have any regard for facts you cannot say that it [the expedition] failed any more than you can as yet say that it was a success." Actually, the conference which developed from the cruise was to labor for a solid year, seeking to halt the war.

The organization of this body was a minor triumph. Hardly had the *Oscar II* docked at Christiania when it was prophesied that Norway would never furnish delegates, while later it was said with equal assurance that no eminent Dutch or Swiss would be available for service. Yet, largely through Lochner's efforts, representatives from six countries, including the United States, were chosen, and by late February, 1916, the Neutral Conference for Continuous Mediation was ready to begin its work.

Meanwhile the feeling against Rosika Schwimmer had continued to grow, the Ford representatives acted to curtail her power, and she finally cabled her resignation. Lochner later discussed her place in the enterprise. She had prodigious capacity for work, "eloquence, wit, *savoir-faire*, forcefulness . . . a genuine personal charm," with an ability to speak English, French, and German fluently. She had enjoyed Ford's confidence. Why did she fail? Lochner concluded that she did so because she was an autocrat and could not adapt herself to the open, frank personalities of the Americans. They (with the Dutch and Scandinavians) despised intrigue; her instinct was to guard her secret documents and work indirectly for what she wanted. She even stationed an agent outside meetings to be sure that nobody eavesdropped!

The conference quickly developed a character and a program. Their first notable act was an appeal in March, 1916, to the neutral powers, urging them to take the initiative in offering mediation. As a result, bills to implement it were introduced in the parliaments of Sweden, Norway, Switzerland, and Holland; but no action was taken by any neutral government.

A month and a half later the conference issued an Appeal to the Governments, Parliaments and Peoples of Belligerent Nations. This document not only again stated the case against continuing the war, but also offered a set of principles which might form the basis for peace. These included the right of self-determination by peoples, guarantees of economic freedom (to make wars for commercial advantage pointless), freedom of the seas, parliamentary control of foreign policy, an international organization to promote co-operation between nations and peaceful settlement for all disputes, and a program of world disarmament. A world congress was to deal with these questions.

After this appeal, on instructions from Dearborn, the five delegates per nation were reduced to two, and the site of sessions was transferred to The Hague. The conference stimulated pro-mediation gatherings, encouraged appeals for peace by eminent writers like Georg Brandes, and indirectly stimulated others like Ellen Key, Selma Lagerlöf, and Arne Carbourg to serve the same end. Representatives of the group communicated with prominent citizens of belligerent countries, suggested that the German government endorse the idea of a league of nations (which it soon did), and planned an international magazine devoted to peace.

Ford meanwhile had vigorously pursued his opposition to war and preparedness through large advertisements in various American newspapers. Apparently he was pleased with the work of the conference in Europe. In October, when Lochner visited the United States, Ford was cordial, but wanted a shift to direct mediatory efforts—contacts with belligerent nationals, attempts to find a common ground for action, and so forth. Lochner was heartened. He felt that all the belligerents were showing a desire to negotiate and that overtures toward action would soon be made, either through the conference or through President Wilson.

An overture soon came, but not in a form that Lochner welcomed. Emperor Wilhelm of Germany announced his willingness to negotiate, but in so arrogant a fashion as to antagonize the Allied governments and peoples. Wilson, who had been about to act, was embarrassed by the imperial gesture. However, apparently eager to be heard before a reply could be made to the Kaiser by others, the President on December 18, 1916, sent to all belligerents notes identical in text suggesting that each declare the terms on which it would consider peace. The Germans promptly expressed a willingness to confer; the Allies rejected the suggestion. Thus two peace tenders (the German and the American) had been made, and their failure had the logical effect of stimulating German activity, including the more intensive use of submarines. This really wrote finis to the activities of the commission (as the conference had become), although as yet no one perceived the fact.

Lochner, still hopeful of peace, was recalled to the United States on January 3, 1917; he saw President Wilson twice and Henry Ford oftener. Wilson made his famous "peace without victory" speech. Ford felt that with this utterance the government had taken over his crusade. As submarine activity assumed a more ruthless character, he also saw the possibility of our being drawn into the war; but apparently his dominant feeling was that Wilson was doing all for peace that he could and more than anyone else could do. On February 7 Lochner was told that the work in Europe would stop.

Thus the peace crusade ended. Having made his decision, Ford could not detach himself from the project too quickly. With his approval, Liebold took over the termination of the work at The Hague, brushing aside Lochner's protest that an abrupt suspension of activities would work hardship upon some of the commission's foreign members and ignoring other suggestions. The drive for peace had lasted fourteen months; what had Ford accomplished in that period?

Opinion on that question varies almost absurdly. Mark Sullivan in *Our Times* declared bitingly of the project: "After its failure, dying down to an echo of gigantic and exhausted laughter, it deprived every other peace movement in the country of force and conviction." Although Sullivan in a footnote reported Jane Addams' vigorous dissent and admitted that the peace movement retained force despite the peace ship, his judgment has been endorsed by some responsible journalists, including Elmer Davis, who reported the cruise, and even historians.

But others have differed sharply. Walter Millis, in his *Road to War*, deplored the fact that "the Peace Ship was launched, to the undying shame of American journalism, upon one vast wave of ridicule." Upton

Ford: "Now you stop!"

Sinclair praised the crusade, while there was scarcely a pilgrim, from Schwimmer to B. W. Huebsch, who did not believe that it justified itself. Those who ridiculed the project had indeed little to support their ridicule, while those who defended it could point to the world-wide dramatization of the peace hope through the cruise and to a definite effect on public opinion in Europe through the activities of the conference. And although the crusade failed, it had held aloft before the world the ever-desirable alternative to war. A large body of Americans respected Ford's idealism, and in less than two years after the conference closed, the industrialist showed amazing strength as a senatorial candidate and was persistently talked of for President.

Ford perceived other practical gains. Although he did not charter the peace ship to make himself or his car better known, the cruise publicized both. When Liebold told him that the total costs were $465,000, he remarked: "Well, we got a million dollars worth of advertising out of it, and a hell of a lot of experience."

Was Ford humbled in spirit by the ridicule he encountered—under which he undoubtedly smarted despite his smiling denials? No evidence supports such a possibility. Later on he pointed out that in a time when no bold effort to end the war was being made, he had acted. "I wanted to see peace. I at least tried to bring it about. Most men did not even try."

The Last Stand of Chief Joseph

CONTINUED FROM PAGE 43

from Idaho to Montana. It was a painful and grueling trip for both pursuers and pursued. The Indian families, stumbling along over steep and rocky trails, guarded by the warriors and driving some 2,000 horses with them, managed to keep well ahead of the troops, who, with their guns and camp equipment, found the going even rougher. In the meantime word of the Indian flight had been telegraphed ahead to Montana, and from Missoula Captain Charles C. Rawn, with 35 men of the 7th Infantry and 200 citizen volunteers from the Bitterroot Valley, hastened to the eastern end of the Lolo Trail and threw up a log fort from which to block the hostiles' passage until Howard could catch up to them from the rear.

On July 25, after nine days in the mountains, the Nez Percés appeared above Rawn's fort, and Joseph, Looking Glass, and an elderly chief named White Bird came down for a parley. Explaining that they were on their way to the Crows, the Indians promised to move peacefully through the Bitterroot Valley, respecting the settlements and paying for any supplies they needed. It satisfied the volunteers, who, having no stomach for an Indian fight, deserted Rawn and stole back to their homes. As a federal officer, Rawn was obliged to continue his posture of resistance, but fortunately for his depleted garrison the Indians shrewdly bypassed his fort and, making a noisy feint in front of him, quietly filed around him on another mountain trail that led them into the Bitterroot Valley. The embarrassed Captain withdrew to Missoula, and his log bastion was promptly dubbed Fort Fizzle by the many wags who were beginning to root for Joseph and the apparently unconquerable Nez Percés.

Moving through the heavily settled valley, the Indians scrupulously maintained their promise to commit no hostile act. At Stevensville they paused to buy coffee, flour, sugar, and tobacco and paid the merchants with gold dust and currency. The friendly treatment they received from the Montana citizens made the Indians believe that, now that they were out of Idaho, the war was over and they were safe. They moved leisurely south to the Big Hole Valley and, on an open meadow beside the willow-lined Big Hole River, pitched camp to rest.

Howard was still far back in the Bitterroots, temporarily out of the picture. But, unknown to the Nez Percés, a new force of 163 army regulars and 35 volunteers under Colonel John Gibbon was hurrying across country from Fort Shaw, on the Sun River, by forced marches to attack them. On the night of August 8 Gibbon gained a wooded hill above the unsuspecting Nez Percé camp and, the next morning at dawn, launched a surprise attack. Firing volleys into the sleeping village, the soldiers charged down the hill in a long line, forded the shallow river, and swept into the camp, shooting and clubbing men, women, and children. Some of the Nez Percés were able to seize their weapons and ammunition belts and escape to the shelter of the willows. There they were rallied by the aged White Bird, who cried at them, "Why are we retreating? Since the world was made, brave men have fought for their women and children! Fight! Shoot them down! We can shoot as well as any of these soldiers!"

Gibbon's commanding officer on the left had been killed during the opening charge and, without a leader, that part of the line faltered as Indians stood their ground and fought back desperately from the tepees. The troopers were forced toward the right, allowing the Nez Percés in that sector to erect a firing line against them. This brought confusion to the main part of the camp, where Gibbon's men, in complete control, were unsuccessfully trying to set the leather tepees afire. With his milling troops being pushed together and soldiers being struck both by the Indians on the left and by White Bird's snipers on the right, Gibbon, who had been wounded in the leg, ordered a withdrawal across the river to the protection of the wooded knoll from which the attack had been launched. To his chagrin the Nez Percés swarmed after him, and in a few moments he found himself on the defensive, fighting fiercely, his position encircled by well-concealed Indian sharpshooters.

As the soldiers pulled out of the village, the old men, women, and children, directed by Joseph, hurried back in, picked up their dead and wounded, struck the tepees, and, driving their pack strings and pony herds ahead of them, moved off toward the south. The warriors remained behind, continuing the siege on the hill throughout the day and into the night, pinning down Gibbon's men in shallow holes and behind fallen trees, and picking off anyone who showed himself. Cut off and without prospect of relief, the soldiers' position rapidly became desperate. The men ran out of water, and cries from the unattended wounded filled the air. Gibbon's howitzer, ordered to come up after the initial attack, arrived on the scene and was immediately captured by a group of wildcharging Nez Percés, who rolled it over a steep bluff. Another body of Indians seized a packload of 2,000 rounds of Gibbon's ammunition. By eleven that night, with their camp safely away, the warriors mercifully decided to break off the engagement and spare the surviving troopers. Backing off slowly to guard against pursuit, they took the trail after Joseph.

Gibbon's men, cut up and dazed, were in no condition to follow. Thirty-three soldiers were dead and thirty-eight wounded. Fourteen of the seventeen officers were casualties. Howard's men, coming up hurriedly the next day, found the troops still in a state of shock, burying the dead and trying to care for the groaning wounded.

The Indians' losses at the Big Hole had also been high. Between sixty and ninety Nez Percés had lost their lives, including Rainbow, Five Wounds, and some of the tribe's most able warriors. Many of the casualties had been women and children, slain during the initial attack on the tepees. Joseph's wife had been among the seriously wounded, and Joseph had been seen fighting his way through the early part of the battle sheltering his new baby in his arms.

The Nez Percés now quickened their retreat across southwestern Montana. Gone were illusions that the whites would let them be. In their desperation to escape, only one haven seemed left to them. Like Sitting Bull, they would go to Canada and seek refuge among the tribes in the country of Queen Victoria. Canada was hundreds of miles away, but they would get there somehow. Looking Glass, blamed for the false sense of security that had led to so many deaths at the Big Hole, was relieved of command, and a tough fighter named Lean Elk, whom the whites had known as Poker Joe, was elevated to supreme chief. The column headed eastward toward Targhee Pass, which would lead the refugees over the Continental Divide to the Yellowstone, where they could turn north to Canada. West of the pass, rear-guard scouts brought word that Howard was catching up and pressing close behind them again. In a bold night attack, 28 warriors led by Ollokot and three other chiefs stole back to Howard's camp and ran off the General's entire pack string. Howard came to a dead halt, forced to scour the settlements for more animals, and the Indians hurried on, unhampered, across the Divide and into the area which five years before had become Yellowstone National Park.

A sight-seeing party, of which General William Tecumseh Sherman was a member, had just left the area, but the Nez Percés swooped up two other groups of campers and took them along. The chiefs insisted on humane treatment for the frightened tourists, who included a number of women. In time, as the Indians continued across the park, past geysers and bubbling mudpots, the sight-seers were allowed to escape. On the eastern side of the park, the Indians found themselves harassed by new bodies of troops, coming at them from posts on the Montana plains. One force of the 7th Cavalry under Colonel Samuel Sturgis tried to set a trap for the Indians in the upper Yellowstone Valley, but the Nez Percés fought their way skillfully through a mountain wilderness where the whites thought passage would be impossible and emerged on the Clark's Fork River in Sturgis' rear. Realizing he had been tricked, Sturgis gave chase with 300 men, following the Indians across the Yellowstone River and down its northern bank past present-day Billings, Montana.

On and on the Indians hurried. Near Canyon Creek they passed a stage station and captured a stagecoach. Letting its occupants escape into some nearby willows, the warriors had a day of great fun, driving the incongruous-looking coach along in the rear of the column. The sport ended abruptly. At Canyon Creek the bands turned north, and here, on September 13, Sturgis' hard-riding cavalry overtook them. There was a furious fight. A rear guard of Indians, hiding behind rocks and in gullies, held off the troopers while the Nez Percé women and children drove the pack strings and herds to the protection of a narrow canyon that cut north through rimrock country. Sturgis ordered his men to dismount, an error that allowed the Indians to escape into the canyon. Later the cavalry tried to follow the Nez Percés in a running fight up the canyon, but the Indians succeeded in making pursuit difficult by blocking the canyon floor behind them with boulders and brush. At darkness, weary and running out of ammunition and rations, Sturgis gave up the chase. Three of his men had been killed and eleven wounded. The Indians counted three wounded, but the long pursuit was beginning to tell heavily on them. They too were becoming tired and dispirited, and they were losing horses. Many of the animals were going lame from the difficult trek and had to be abandoned. Others were being lost in the hurry to keep moving.

Beyond Canyon Creek their old allies, the Crows, now in service as scouts for the army, began to attack them. The Nez Percés fought them off in running engagements and continued across the Musselshell to the Missouri River, helping themselves to army stores at a military depot on Cow Island while a frightened sergeant and twelve men looked on helplessly from behind an earthwork. Just across the Missouri, the Indians fought off a half-hearted attack by a small force from Fort Benton and hastened on across badlands and open, rolling plains to the Bear Paw Mountains. About thirty miles short of the Canadian line, exhausted by the long flight, they paused to rest, confident that they had outdistanced all pursuers.

Once more they were wrong, outflanked again by

the telegraph, and this time the pause would end in their last stand. From Fort Keogh in the east, Colonel Nelson A. Miles, with nearly 600 men that included the 2nd and 7th Cavalry, the mounted 5th Infantry, and a body of Cheyenne warriors, was hastening obliquely across Montana, hoping to intercept the hostiles before they crossed the border. On the cold, blustery morning of September 30, Miles's Cheyenne scouts sighted the Nez Percé tepees in a deep hollow on the plains close to Snake Creek on the northern edge of the Bear Paw Mountains. Miles ordered an immediate attack, and the Cheyennes and 7th Cavalry, supported by the 5th Infantry, charged across the open ground toward the village.

The assault caught the Nez Percés in three groups. Some, including women and children, were on the distant side of the camp and were able to mount and flee to the north, where they scattered on the broken plains, to die from hunger and exposure or to eventually reach Canada in small, pitiful groups. Others, including Joseph, were trapped with the horses at some distance from the camp. A third group, at the village, found protection behind a low-lying ridge. These warriors, hidden behind rocks, opened a deadly fire on the attackers, inflicting heavy casualties and sending the troopers reeling back short of the camp. Two officers and twenty-two soldiers were killed in the assault and four officers and thirty-eight enlisted men wounded.

The 2nd Cavalry, meanwhile, had been sent around the camp to capture the Nez Percé pony herd and try to cut off escape. This unit had better luck. The troopers crashed into the herd, stampeding the horses and splitting the Indians into small groups that fought back hand-to-hand or sought cover in gullies or behind rocks. A few of the Indians got away on ponies and disappeared to the north. Others, among them Joseph, crawled or fought their way back to the main body of Nez Percés, reaching the camp under cover of darkness. The troopers drove off at least a third of the horses, however, and most of the Nez Percés' remaining war leaders, including the brave Ollokot and Toohoolhoolzote, were killed in the fighting.

The heavy casualties Miles had sustained deterred him from ordering another charge, and he decided to lay siege to the village. He made one attempt to cut off the Indians from their water supply by establishing a line between the camp and the river, but the troops detailed to the task were driven back by fierce Indian resistance. As the siege settled down, both sides dug in, continuing a desultory sharpshooting fire between the lines. The weather turned bitterly cold, and the next morning five inches of snow covered the unretrieved bodies of the dead. The Indians, wounded, hungry, and cold, suffered intensely. Using hooks, knives, and

pans, the people tried to dig crude shelters in the sides of the hollows. One dugout was caved in by a hit from Miles's howitzer that had been tilted back for use as a mortar, and a woman and child were buried alive.

As the siege continued, Miles grew concerned. There were rumors that Sitting Bull, with a band of Sioux, was coming to the Nez Percés' rescue from Canada. And, even if they didn't show up, Howard was getting closer, and Miles wanted the glory of Joseph's end for himself. Hoping to hurry the surrender, he hoisted a white flag over his trenches and, after negotiations with a Nez Percé who could speak English, lured Joseph across the lines. The two men parlayed amicably for a few moments, but when Joseph began to detail terms for an honorable surrender, Miles had him seized and made prisoner. The same day, however, the Nez Percés captured one of Miles's officers. The next morning an exchange was agreed to, and Joseph was returned to his camp.

The siege went on amid cold and snow flurries, and on October 4 Howard reached the battlefield with a small advance party that included two treaty Nez Percés. The appearance of their old enemy, heralding the arrival of reinforcements for Miles, took the final heart out of the suffering Nez Percés. The next morning the two treaty Nez Percés crossed the lines and told the chiefs that if they surrendered, they would be honorably treated and sent back to Lapwai. The chiefs held a final council. White Bird and Looking Glass still opposed surrender. Joseph pointed to the starving women and children in the shelter pits and to the babies that were crying around them. "For myself I do not care," he said. "It is for them I am going to surrender."

As the council broke up, Looking Glass was suddenly struck in the forehead by a stray bullet and killed. As the surviving warriors gathered around the slain chief, Joseph mounted a horse and, followed by several men on foot, rode slowly up the hill from the camp and across to the army lines where Howard and Miles awaited him. As he reached the officers, he dismounted and handed Miles his rifle. Then, stepping back, he adjusted his blanket to leave his right arm free and, addressing Miles, began one of the most touching and beautiful speeches of surrender ever made:

"Tell General Howard I know his heart. What he told me before I have in my heart. I am tired of fighting. Our chiefs are killed. Looking Glass is dead. Toohoolhoolzote is dead. The old men are all dead. It is the young men who say yes or no. He who led the young men is dead. It is cold and we have no blankets. The little children are freezing to death. My people,

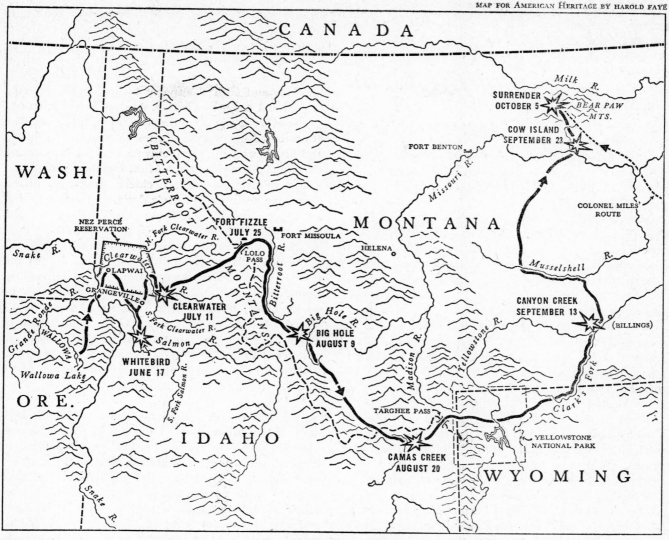

The Nez Percé retreat covered 1,300 miles in about four months. Miles cut them off just short of Canada and safety.

some of them, have run away to the hills, and have no blankets, no food; no one knows where they are—perhaps freezing to death. I want to have time to look for my children and see how many I can find. Maybe I shall find them among the dead. Hear me, my chiefs. I am tired; my heart is sick and sad. From where the sun now stands, I will fight no more forever."

The fact that neither Joseph nor any other individual chief had been responsible for the outstanding strategy and masterful successes of the campaign is irrelevant. The surrender speech, taken down by Howard's adjutant and published soon afterwards, confirmed Joseph in the public's mind as the symbol of the Nez Percés' heroic, fighting retreat. Although the government failed to honor Miles's promise to send the Indians back to Lapwai, sympathy was aroused throughout the nation for Joseph's people. At first the

Indians were shipped by flatboats and boxcars to unfamiliar, hot country in the Indian Territory, where many of them sickened and died. But friendly whites and sympathetic societies in the East continued to work for them, and public sentiment finally forced approval of their return to the Northwest. In 1885 Joseph and most of his band were sent to the Colville Reservation in Washington. Joseph made many attempts to be allowed to resettle in the Wallowa but each time was rebuffed. In 1904 he died, broken-hearted, an exile from the beautiful valley he still considered home.

Alvin M. Josephy, Jr., an associate editor of Time, *is currently working on a history of the Northwest. This is Mr. Josephy's third article in* AMERICAN HERITAGE.

The three paintings (pp. 37-43) are part of a series of miniature historical oils executed by Olaf C. Seltzer, Danishborn painter of the American West.

The Yankee
and the Czar

CONTINUED FROM PAGE 9

in Caulaincourt's private theater. From this, Adams got home at 2 A.M.

He met the grand dukes and grand duchesses at stiff palace receptions where conversation also centered on the weather ("How does Mrs. Adams support the climate of the country?" Alexander's empress asked him), but he was more intrigued by the phenomenal Princess Woldemar Galitzin, who was "venerable by the length and thickness of her beard." Adams had understood that beards were known among women "of Slavonian breed," but the Princess, he thought, "of all the females I have ever seen [is] the one who most resembles a Grecian philosopher."

Mrs. Adams, being pregnant, was often unable to accompany her husband on his evening rounds, which reached their midwinter height at a gay torchlight party given by Caulaincourt at his country retreat. To this the Ambassador had invited some fifty friends to enjoy sliding down his "ice-hills" with their ladies. Most of them came "specially equipped for the purpose," Adams recorded in his diary, the men in heavy pantaloons, the ladies in fur-lined riding habits. Together, after a magnificent dinner at 4 P.M., they coasted on their posteriors while servants with lamps and torches lighted the way.

Adams' custom had always been to rise early—never later than six—and begin the day with an hour's reading of the Bible. Yet here "we rise seldom before nine in the morning—often not before ten. . . . The night parties seldom break up until four or five in the morning. It is a life of such irregularity and dissipation as I cannot and will not continue to lead."

But he did, regarding it as his duty to meet everyone and miss nothing. On the empress mother's birthday, festivities began with a formal court at noon, followed by a *cercle* that lasted until three. Then, after dinner, back to the palace for an opera at the adjoining Hermitage, followed by still another reception and the viewing of fireworks on the river. Easter Eve brought a late night in another vein. At midnight, as cannons heralded the coming of Easter, the imperial family and the whole court entered the palace chapel, each person carrying a lighted taper, while the choir in red-laced robes chanted a processional. After the ceremony of kissing sacred relics, the Czar embraced a whole line of priests, his mother then doing the same. Then the Czar embraced his mother, and all the grand dukes

in turn embraced him and her. Thereupon the Chancellor, the grand chamberlains, and the officers of court also kissed the relics and the Czar's hand, the chanting going on continually for an hour. Finally, as Adams stood astonished, the massed noblemen "turned to one another, and such a scene of kissing and embracing ensued as I never saw before. As they passed from one to the other it was a continual motion, like a beehive. It reminded me of a description in Ariosto of a Sultan and his Court falling suddenly into a fit of involuntary dancing." After that, High Mass. Home at 3 A.M.

The minister of Austria, elderly Count St. Julien, then gave a dinner in a style designed to rival that of the French ambassador. Footmen lined the antechambers and stood behind each place at table. Rare delicacies such as pineapple were served. During dinner a band played so loudly upon horns, drums, and cymbals as to make conversation almost impossible. Count St. Julien was, unfortunately, half-deaf: he couldn't hear how loud his band was. Adams: "I observed the rule of temperance better than usual, to which I believe the stunning noise of the music in some contributed. For by preventing all conversation it left my mind unoccupied by anything which could lead me to forget my resolution."

No one, actually, could hope to vie with the brilliant Caulaincourt. A favorite of Napoleon ever since his own mistress had become lady in waiting to Empress Josephine, he lived in St. Petersburg at an annual outlay of about one million rubles (well over $300,000 at that time, and the equivalent of perhaps $1,500,000 now) and was served by over sixty retainers and a comparable number of horses. Adams wrote his mother, Abigail, in Boston what a dinner at the Frenchman's was like. At the door you were greeted by a gold-laced porter, then ushered upstairs by some twenty footmen, saluted by a pair of *chasseurs* in green and silver, escorted through antechambers by a line of higher servants, then welcomed by a succession of secretaries before being received by the Ambassador himself.

After appetizers in the inner *salon*, the fifty-odd guests filed into the dining room to sit down to a succession of seven or eight courses of rising novelty before the main one was reached. Different wines were served with every dish, the butlers whispering to each guest the year of the vintage and the name of the vineyard. For the *pièce de résistance* precious Sèvres porcelain was laid and fresh napkins of the finest damask were presented. Then came the champagne, preserves, fruits, and ices, accompanied by small glasses of dessert wine. After this, frozen punch, and later, English porter and ale. The whole massive dinner, Adams wrote home, was served in little more than an hour by attendants moving like clockwork, and, he found, "there is less of intemperance in fifty such feasts than in one of our dinners succeeded by a carousal of six hours long, swilling upon a mixture of madeira wine and brandy."

In such an environment Adams could not hope to compete financially, and at one point his mother, worried about his expenses, wrote President Madison suggesting that he bring her son home. Friends offered loans to the Minister, but Adams replied that he must stick to his principles and live within his income. Everyone at court, even the Czar himself, knew that the American representative was strapped for funds. Not that he was living in penury. Adams' salary was $9,000 (again, equivalent to possibly five times that much today), a sum exceeded at home only by that paid to the President himself; in addition, he had received on departure another $9,000 for expenses. His establishment included a maître d'hôtel, or steward; a cook and two Russian helpers; a Swiss porter; two footmen; "a mujik to make the fires"; a coachman and a postilion; a Negro valet; an American chambermaid; a personal maid for Mrs. Adams; a housemaid and a laundry helper. When he went out to dine, he did so in a style he termed "altogether republican," although by this he meant that he went in a coach-and-four, attended by his two footmen in livery, the coachman on the box, and his postilion on the right-side horse of the leading pair.

But it was not Adams' excursions in a coach-and-four that made his success in Russia. It was his daytime habit of going out on walks alone. The Czar, an unconventional man himself, liked also to go out walking alone. Adams soon discovered where Alexander liked most to walk, namely, along the embankment of the Neva, and this led to a series of sidewalk encounters of increasing intimacy—all presumably accidental —between monarch and minister.

Only an ambassador had the right of direct access to the sovereign, and the only diplomat of that rank then at St. Petersburg was Napoleon's Caulaincourt. Adams, almost the least of ministers, was expected to conduct his business with the Chancellery. The only error in this hierarchic calculation was that Napoleon's envoy did not go out walking.

Often the talk at Adams' riverside meetings with the Czar revolved merely about that perennial St. Petersburg subject, the weather. Alexander apologized for its severity and hoped that Mr. Adams would not have "too bad an opinion" of it, to which Adams responded diplomatically that he thought highly of cold climates. One frosty day the Czar noticed that Adams was out walking without gloves, to which Adams replied that

he wore them only in extreme temperatures. This led to a discussion of the merits of opening one's windows to the cold night air and of wearing flannel pajamas. The Czar inquired solicitously about Mrs. Adams' confinement. He was also interested in learning more about a young American named Jones who had already made two trips to this part of Europe, which struck him as remarkable, since "such a voyage is not like crossing the Neva." Adams answered pleasantly yet meaningfully in French, "My countrymen, Sire, are so familiarized with the ocean that they think not much more of crossing it than of going over a river."

The Czar began to look forward to these man-to-man encounters, even though the two rarely touched upon the urgent matters uppermost in their minds. One evening at a ball, Alexander remarked to Adams that he had missed him that day on their promenade: had he kept to his house? No, Adams hadn't. But he had gone out without his court wig, which possibly had caused the Czar to fail to recognize him. This led to some banter about wigs, which Adams hated wearing. The upshot was that he felt himself exempted from wearing one even at court and never did again.

The court asked itself just what had been said at these unusual meetings. "Minister Adams' influence here has an element of the mysterious," remarked a visiting Frenchwoman, the Countess de Choiseul. Yet all Adams had really been doing was to keep before the Czar's mind the image of himself and the nation he represented—this at a time when the Czar had become so harassed he was not sure he knew his own mind.

On one hand Alexander was beholden to his French ally, and on the other, he was becoming increasingly restive. For one thing, Russia needed foreign commerce, and the neutral Americans were now its chief carriers. The French branded the Americans as virtual partners of Britain, demonstrating that many of our ships touched at British ports and even sailed in British convoy. True; yet Yankee shippers were offering needed staples and good money for Russia's own. Adams spoke incessantly of this commerce, stressing first its rights and then its opportunities. His manner conveyed conviction and strength, and Alexander intensely admired strength.

Within a few months of his arrival, Adams' persistence bore first fruit. The Czar made representations to the Danes about their stoppage of American ships. In doing so he interfered directly in the affairs of one of Napoleon's allies. All next spring, as Baltic ports reopened, Adams pursued his case. That summer he told the State Department that the issue of commerce was threatening to disrupt the Russo-French alliance.

In the fall he sharply lectured Caulaincourt, hoping that the French would still mend their policy. "You will do us immense injury; you will oppress the continent of Europe and yourselves with it; but take my word for it, and I pray you three years hence to remember what I say, you will do England more good than harm."

Caulaincourt smiled, but Adams' prediction came true. That winter the Czar, determined at last to free himself of French dominance, issued a ukase freely admitting American ships to his ports and at the same time virtually blocking French produce from them. Adams informed the secretary of state in code that Russia's new determination seemed "fixed and unalterable." It was more than that. It was revolutionary, and it helped lead to war.

Napoleon angrily recalled Caulaincourt, charging his favorite with a lack of diligence and with having become "mesmerized" by the Czar. Before the outmaneuvered ambassador left, he had sharp exchanges with Adams. "Your ships have done a great deal of business here on English account," he charged. Adams retorted that Americans worked for themselves; and, "Thanks to you, we have had scarcely any part of the continent of Europe open to us." In the end, though, the departing Frenchman took Adams' hand and congratulated him on his professional success. "It seems you are great favorites here; you have found powerful protection."

That spring some two hundred American ships swarmed into the Baltic. Adams relaxed to reread the Bible, Cicero, and Massillon's sermons and to measure the sun's inclination at the solstice. Then, one day in March, 1812, he again met the Czar on the blustery quay. The usually affable monarch was somber. "And so it is, after all, that war is coming which I have done so much to avoid," he blurted. "Napoleon keeps pushing forward. Now he can't advance any further without attacking us." Several regiments of the St. Petersburg garrison had already been moved to the frontier. The following month, monarch and minister met once more on the embankment, and this time the Czar's expression was even more cheerless. Adams knew that Alexander was about to join his army in the field. They talked only about the weather. It was the last time they met.

The *Grande Armée* rolled in across the Niemen, and St. Petersburg promptly suppressed all news of military movements. "Great anxiety here," Adams noted in July; "rumors of disasters both to Prince Bagration's army and to that of the Emperor himself." Then the government began putting out optimistic reports. Adams was told that "the French army is wedged in between the first and second Russian armies, and in an extremely dangerous position." He attended a *Te Deum* at the great Church of Our Lady of Kazan and there saw the barrel-shaped figure of General Kutuzov, hero of the late war against the Turks.

COLLECTION OF NATHANIEL SPEAR, JR.

NAPOLEON I
The Czar's inconstant ally

August brought another *Te Deum* with bell-ringing, cannon salutes, and illuminations because of a supposed victory around Smolensk. Yet the French kept advancing. General Kutuzov was hurried forward to take command of both Russian armies. Adams watched new levies being ordered up, many of them serfs of the nobility: "I saw many of them this morning, just in from the country, with the one-horse wagons, and the families of the recruits taking leave of them." In late September he heard the first rumors of the capture of Moscow. There had been no battle reported since that at Borodino, "which Kutuzov reported as a splendid victory, for which he was made a Field Marshal and received from the Emperor a present of 100,000 rubles. The result of this great Russian victory was to put the French in possession of Moscow."

Dark gloom now descended upon the capital. It was thought that Napoleon's next objective would be St. Petersburg. The days grew short and the weather more severe. Yet Adams, again prophetically, wrote his father, "Napoleon is in an enemy's country, hemmed in between four Russian armies over whose bodies he must either advance or retreat; two thousand miles distant from his own capital; having lost one half the forces with which he commenced the war; and surrounded in the midst of his camp by auxiliary armies so disaffected . . . that at the first symptom of defeat they would more eagerly turn their arms against him than they now follow his banners."

Then came the bells of another *Te Deum*—a dubious sound to an American already highly suspicious of *Te Deums*. Moscow had been liberated! November brought still another *Te Deum* to honor the defeat of Davoust's and Ney's corps, Davoust's baton being exhibited in the church beside the icons as a trophy. A few days later Adams dined at Chancellor Romanzoff's in a festive company that included the wives of Kutuzov and his chief field commanders—not including the greatest of them all, the one whom Napoleon had

CAULAINCOURT
Napoleon's free-spending envoy

called "General Winter." That day it was reported that forty to fifty thousand shivering *Grand Armée* prisoners had been brought in. In St. Petersburg the cold became so fierce, even indoors, that for seventeen days on end Adams could hardly hold a pen in hand. Yet Russian spirits were exuberant, and soon it became known that Napoleon had abandoned his broken army in headlong flight, coaching home over snows with only one companion—Caulaincourt.

After a climactic thanksgiving in the Kazan sanctuary, at which Adams was amazed to see all the Czar's family prostrate themselves utterly, Russia buried obese Marshal Kutuzov, dead after his exertions, surrounded by captured eagles and with the huge figure of an angel suspended from the dome on a rope holding a crown of laurel over the two-ton catafalque.

Yet there was more for the American minister to do than simply witness history in procession. There was human comedy no less than tragedy to be observed. There were Americans, like the steamboat inventor Robert Fulton, to be assisted. There was Mme de Staël. And there was the inconvenient war newly broken out between the United States and England to be justified and prevented from growing into a bigger war.

One day, amid the deadly Russian clash with Napoleon, Adams took time to notice that the new British ambassador had been so overcome by weariness at a long reception in the chairless Throne Room of the Winter Palace that he simply stretched out on one edge of the imperial dais and went to sleep. Another day, Mrs. Adams learned from Countess Colombi that one Baroness Koscull, "alias Mrs. Hall," had gone into the business of fortunetelling and had foretold so much that the chief of police had paid her a visit and advised her not to be so knowing.

Then, in the war's darkest days, came a request from the ambitious Fulton, fresh from his success on the Hudson with his *Clermont,* that Adams procure him a monopoly for steamboat operation on Russian rivers, too. Adams, always anxious to promote American enterprise, composed a note to the Chancellor in his best French, beginning, "Le Sieur Robert Fulton, citoyen des Etats Unis, est l'inventeur d'une espèce de chaloupe ou navire pour naviguer sur les rivières, même contre les vents et les courants par le moyen du feu et de la vapeur . . ." He went on to say that Fulton and his partner Robert R. Livingston, having proved their success with a vessel able to steam in as little as 24 hours from New York to Albany ("a distance of 240 *versts*") would like a twenty-year franchise in Russia also. "Can Fulton's vessels stem rapids as well as currents?" the Chancellor asked dubiously—although few Russian rivers had rapids. Adams had to confess that so far as he knew, they couldn't—and there the matter rested.

Then, also in mid-war, came Mme de Staël, a fugitive from Napoleon and bent on overwhelming St. Petersburg with her conversation as well as her fame as Europe's greatest *femme fatale.* "She talks in folios," Lord Byron had said of her; "she should have been a man." Yet a trail of famous love affairs all across Europe testified to her femininity. The French emperor had tried to have her silenced as a libertarian bent on destroying his regime. Within a fortnight of reaching the Russian capital, she invited Adams to come and see her.

Although America by then was at war with Britain, Adams was received in her *salon* together with the British envoy and veteran Admiral Bentinck of the Royal Navy, with both of whom he still mixed socially —such were the forms of the times—and then was treated to a long monologue by his hostess praising the British nation as the world's greatest civilizing force since antiquity. When the famous woman finally ended her oration, bluff Admiral Bentinck muttered to Adams, "Thank God, that is finished," and took his leave with the others, leaving the American alone with Mme de Staël. Then began a duel between Europe's leading freethinker and free liver and the Boylston Street Puritan that ranged from topics such as religion (for which she had little use) and international morality (of which she claimed herself an apostle) to American and British policy. "How was it possible that America should have declared war on England?" she demanded. "Why didn't America join in the holy cause against Napoleon?"

Adams fixed the bosomy, slightly untidy presence and answered crisply, "First, because we have no means for making war against him. Secondly, because it is a fundamental maxim of American policy not to intermeddle with the political affairs of Europe. Thirdly, because it is altogether unnecessary. He has enemies enough upon his hands already."

"What! Don't you dread his universal monarchy?"

"Not in the least, madam. I don't believe and never

85

have that he would subjugate even the continent of Europe. If there ever was a real danger of such an event, it is past."

"Everything you say of Napoleon is very just," she finally heaved. "But I have particular reasons for resentment against him. I have been persecuted by him in the most shameful manner . . . for no good reason but because I would not eulogize him in my writings."

Next day Adams called on her again. Before she took off for her next stop at Stockholm, she asked him to be sure to visit her wherever their paths might cross once more, which he promised to do. To his father at home he wrote, "Whom can one help deserting for Mme de Staël?"

When Adams had first arrived in St. Petersburg, Russia was fighting Britain in league with France, and America had seemed London's tacit ally. Now America was fighting Britain on her own over rights at sea, while Russia in turn was fighting France and was in growing accord with maritime Britain. All of this left St. Petersburg looking upon Adams as being in cahoots with the hostile French. In this international whirligig Adams kept both his senses and his humor, insisting that no matter what either changing side did, Americans had no reason to fall out with our imperial Russian friends—a sentiment Czar Alexander reciprocated when he proposed that he himself mediate the Anglo-American war before it had hardly begun. The British first disdained this proposal, then seemed willing to toy with it—and, although the unstable Czar himself backed away from it, his intervention led to the equitable settlement we finally reached with the British at Ghent, of which John Quincy Adams himself was chief architect.

Schoolbooks today still tend to present this second Adams as a somewhat dour patriot who emerged on the stage with that treaty, then wrote the Monroe Doctrine, and finally became our starchiest statesman and one of our least personable Presidents. Yet there was also an Adams who became a superbly rounded, human, and effective American—in St. Petersburg.

William Harlan Hale, who wrote "When Karl Marx Worked for Horace Greeley" for our April, 1957, issue, is a contributing editor of The Reporter. *He is now at work on a book about distinguished Americans abroad throughout history.*

Classmates Divided CONTINUED FROM PAGE 35

known to his fellow cadets as "Rip." He died commanding the guns of a North Carolina battery on July 3.

The artillery seems to have been particularly unhealthy at Gettysburg. Lieutenant Malbone Watson of the 5th Regular Artillery, a member of the May class of 1861, took a bad wound in his right leg on Little Round Top on July 2. A few moments later his classmate Charles Edward Hazlett bent down to catch the final orders of Brigadier General Stephen Weed, who was dying beside Watson's guns. As he bent over his commander, Hazlett took a bullet through the brain and fell dead on Weed's body.

The June class of 1861 also had cause to remember that second day at Gettysburg. Patrick Henry O'Rorke had headed the class of which Custer ingloriously occupied the foot. At Gettysburg he led the 140th New York Infantry. On his way to the field he halted the regiment and addressed it briefly; he expected every man to do his duty, and if any man failed, the file-closers would shoot him! In the famous struggle for Little Round Top—at just about the time Watson and Hazlett got hit—he led the 140th up that craggy little hill just in time to repulse a Confederate charge, got a bullet in the throat, and fell dead.

On July 3 at Gettysburg, at the precise part of the Union line which Pickett's famous charge was getting ready to hit, there were two batteries of regular artillery, each commanded by a member of the old June class. One was George Augustus Woodruff, who was put out of action by a serious wound just before the great charge got started; the other was Alonzo H. Cushing, a slender, almost girlish young lieutenant who was only sixteen when he entered the Military Academy and who was a cadet captain when he graduated.

On that third day at Gettysburg the Union line was pierced, through no fault of Alonzo Cushing's. He fought while his limbers were blown up and his caissons shot to matchwood. He fought while his guns were disabled one by one. He fought while his gunners died at his side. He was wounded, bandaged the wounds, and fought on. His second in command was killed. Every other officer in the battery was gone. Cushing took a ball through his right shoulder. Still he refused to leave his guns. White to the lips from loss of blood, he ordered Sergeant Fuger to hold him on his feet.

He fell into Fuger's arms, wounded again. This time the shrapnel had torn open the lower part of his abdomen. That was a mortal wound, but Cushing clamped his left arm against his torn belly, struggled

Members of the 1861 classes were among the cadets who passed in review—at the double —when the Prince of Wales (in top hat, center) visited West Point in October of 1860.

to his feet, and continued to whisper perfectly rational orders to his frantic sergeant.

At last only a single gun was left. It was triple-charged with canister—the very last of the battery's ammunition. The few remaining men managed to run it down to the wall. As Alonzo Cushing jerked the lanyard, a bullet sped between his parted lips and slammed into the base of his brain. The sergeant laid him on the bloody grass, just as the Confederate General Lewis Armistead leaped on the wall, put his hand on the still-smoking gun, and then fell mortally wounded beside it.

Early on the afternoon of July 4, George Woodruff died of his wound in a little stone school house two miles behind the lines. On that same day the surgeons cut off Malbone Watson's right leg; he would return to West Point, on recovery, to teach French at the academy during the rest of the war.

All of these men, and many others like them, are commemorated in the great Battle Monument which towers above the plain at West Point—the one memorial *to* men of the Regular Army built with contributions *from* men of the Regular Army. Nearly a century has passed since the site of that monument was dedicated. Far below it, the Hudson flows on its endless course; on the plain around it, the academy classes come and go, and down the marching years a few return to the scene . . .

> *To our comrades who have fallen,*
>   *one cup before we go;*
> *They poured their life-blood freely out,*
>   pro bono publico.
> *No marble points the stranger*
>   *to where they rest below—*
> *They lie neglected far away*
>   *from Benny Havens Oh!*

Many do lie far away from the paths their youthful steps climbed. George Woodruff's body was taken back to Michigan; Justin Dimick sleeps in Portsmouth, New Hampshire, within sound of the restless sea; John Pelham lies among the blue hills of his Alabama home; and Tom Rosser slumbers at Charlottesville, far from his old roommate. But they all seem to linger in the place they all loved. The bones of Custer came back from the shallow grave along the Little Big Horn and lie at West Point, and not far away there is a headstone of the type a class buys for someone whom it really loved. This stone, with a cross at the top, has an inscription:

BREVET LT. COLONEL
ALONZO H. CUSHING
4TH ARTILLERY
FELL
JULY 3RD, 1863,
AT
GETTYSBURG

There are three more words on this white stone, words which might well stand above the headstone of everybody who once marched with the two classes of 1861, and it matters very little whether he wore a blue uniform or a gray one, once he came down from the wind-swept plain—three terrible but beautiful words:

"Faithful unto death."

Mary Elizabeth Sergent has long been interested in the story of John Pelham and his classmates. She is currently engaged in writing a novel based on Pelham's life.

Picture credits, page 30: United States Military Academy Archives; page 31: Pelham—Mary Pelham Graves Collection; Wheeler—United States Military Academy Archives; Lee, Rosser, Ramseur—Confederate Museum.

The Charleston Tradition

CONTINUED FROM PAGE 50

Charleston's aristocracy got its start, however, at the mudsill level. The story of Judith Manigault is essentially that of all the Huguenot families who came to espouse the idea of excellence. Born in Languedoc, France, she had made a daring escape to England via Holland. She married Noé Royer, a weaver, who like Judith had escaped from France in order to gain religious freedom. She and Royer worked the land and cut timber in the swamps and forests; together they operated a whipsaw. For periods of more than half a year at a time, this pioneer couple never saw bread. After the death of Royer, Judith married Pierre Manigault, who also had fled France not many years before. Pierre purchased a small building and took in lodgers. Then, while his new wife managed this humble enterprise, he built a distillery and a cooperage. After a time, he owned warehouses and retail stores in Charleston, and when he died in 1729 his son Gabriel inherited substantial property. Gabriel Manigault developed trade with the West Indies, England, and France. He invested large sums in plantations. When he too was gathered to his fathers, this second-generation Huguenot was one of the three wealthiest men in America. He owned 47,532 acres and 490 slaves. At the age of 75 he enlisted in the Revolutionary forces. Perhaps more important for the cause was his loan to the South Carolina Revolutionary government of $220,000, of which he recovered only about $40,000.

Such was the enterprising breed from which was created the "aristocracy" that Lord Ashley had sought for the province.

In the meanwhile, one casual act by one man, Dr. Woodward, the early arrival who had befriended the Indians, shaped the life of Charleston. In the late 1680's, a Captain John Thurber, master of a New England brigantine, put into Charleston harbor. He became friendly with Woodward and presented him with a packet of Madagascar rice. Fortunately for the city and the generations to come, Woodward planted the rice instead of eating it. In the proper season, the rice sprouted; Woodward gave some of his harvest to friends; they, in turn, planted the rice on their lands; and the city-state had been committed to a way of life.

Rice provided what any great society must have, namely, a firm economic base. Indeed the land of the Carolina Low Country was virtually foreordained to rice growing: the ruling-class mentality, the plantation system from the West Indies, the Negroes to cultivate the land—the seed dropped in fertile social soil. By 1696 the rice harvest was so considerable that there was difficulty finding vessels in which to transport it. Rice built most of Charleston and educated generations of its sons. Rice provided the essential link between city and back country.

Charleston became the capital of the plantations. Its families were country families, but country families were also Charleston families. They spent part of each year—the cool, fever-free months—at their plantations and part in the city. The great work of rice planting went on even in the heart of the city. A story about Daniel Ravenel of Wantoot plantation, whose city house still stands on Broad Street and is occupied by another Daniel Ravenel, illustrates this point. Often during the malaria season Mr. Ravenel's overseer would arrive, seeking the latest planting instructions. The rugs would be rolled back in the drawing room fronting on Broad Street, across from St. Michael's Church, and Mr. Ravenel, using chalk, would trace the rice squares on the polished wood floor, indicating which were to be drained, which flooded.

In time the Carolina Low Country became the "Rice Coast," and the planter ideal, embodied in men like Ravenel, became fixed early in the development of Charleston. The word "planter" was more than a descriptive term—it was an honorable term, almost a title. The ideal involved the whole man, almost in the Renaissance sense. The planter of the eighteenth century was expected to have a splendid versatility, which in fact he often possessed. Planters built houses that rank with the most beautiful in America, raised families on remote sea islands in the midst of African slaves, imported flowering shrubs from Europe and the West Indies, laid out splendid formal gardens, bred race horses, sent their sons to England for their educations, imported European artisans to decorate their homes, prided themselves on their ability as hunters, laid in fine private libraries and actually read the books they bought.

While the families of Charleston thus raised themselves by their bootstraps into a New World aristocracy, they had none of the English notion that business was not an aristocrat's business. Many of the greatest planters were planter-merchants. They carried on an immensely profitable trade with the Indians. They had a healthy respect for money-making skills.

All the physical evidence of Charleston indicates a vastly pleasant life among the planters. They built well; they spoke well. Their letters, portraits, houses, churches, silver plate, and furniture all testify to their vigor and sense of style. They were pleased with their

88

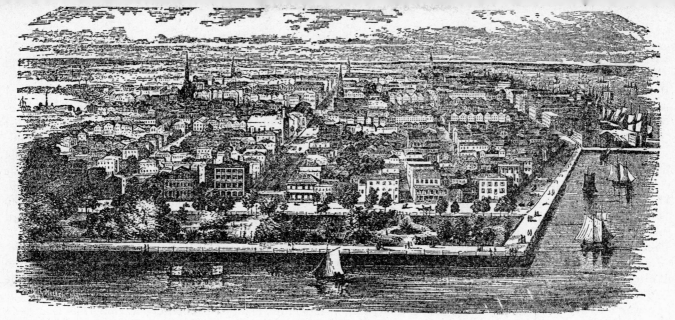

Charleston in 1855 was a prosperous city of 43,000 noted for its people's "refinement, intelligence and hospitality" and the "airy, Oriental appearance" of its homes. Behind the park is South Battery; at right toward the wharves is East Battery.

progress, and proud. In fact, by 1719, Charleston could rebel against the Lords Proprietors. Her people demanded an end to interference with their political liberties. The city declared itself part of a royal province, and ten years later the declaration became an accomplished fact.

The years after the breakaway from the Proprietary government saw an astonishing prosperity in Charleston, based not only on rice but also on a new plant, indigo. War between England and France brought a boon to the planters, for it meant that English weavers were deprived of their customary supplies of the blue dyestuff from French possessions in the West Indies. In 1749 Parliament granted a bounty of sixpence a pound and very successfully stimulated the production of indigo. One South Carolina historian has estimated that indigo did more to enrich the people of the province than the mines of South America for the king of Spain.

Wealth also came from the forests to the west. Beginning with Henry Woodward, Charleston's pathfinders had penetrated far into the American wilderness, opening vast areas of the South to commerce. From trading houses on East Bay Street pack trains set out each year, laden with goods for the Indian trade. In the mid-years of the eighteenth century, Charleston exported annually more than 100,000 deerskins from the back country. Such was the prosperity that a new royal governor, arriving in Charleston in 1743 in the midst of a boom, thought the city much too fond of luxury. He expressed concern because "there are annually imported into this Province considerable Quantities of fine *Flanders Laces,* the finest *Dutch Linens,* and *French Cambricks, Chintz, Hyson Tea,*

and other *East India* Goods, *Silks, Gold* and *Silver Lace,* &c."

An English surgeon visiting Charleston twenty years later was impressed to find "about eleven Hundred Dwelling Houses in the Town, built with Wood or Brick; many of them have a genteel Appearance, though generally incumbered with Balconies or Piazzas; and are always decently, and often elegantly, furnished . . ."

Of the inhabitants he wrote, "Their Complexion is little different from the Inhabitants of *Britain,* and they are generally of a good stature and well made, with lively and agreeable Countenances; sensible, spirited, and open-hearted, and exceed most People in Acts of Benevolence, Hospitality and Charity. The Men and Women who have a Right to the Class of Gentry (who are more numerous here than in any other colony in *North America*) dress with Elegance and Neatness." The ladies he found to be "fond of Dancing . . . and many sing well, and play upon the Harpsichord and Guitar with great Skill." Yet at this time it was only a few miles to the Low Country and a wilderness infested with Indians and alligators.

Charleston was wealthy, with a kind of life no other city in the South save New Orleans was ever to attain. Virginia, for all its glittering plantation society on the James River, was never to know the rich, cultivated city life. Williamsburg was an elegant village but always a village. Richmond's brief flowering as a city came in the days of the Confederacy. Charleston, however, offered city life from the early days of the eighteenth century. In 1736 this pleasure-loving capital saw its first theater built on Dock Street. And London players crossed the ocean to give the planters and their wives a taste of London drama.

Charleston families sent their sons to England and the Continent to be educated and to "mix with their equals." General Charles Cotesworth Pinckney, writing in 1819, gave this account of Carolinians trained in England:

"My father carried his family to England for their education in the year 1753. At that time I remember that . . . John Rutledge and Arthur Middleton were already there. With me went my brother . . . Wm. Henry Drayton, his brother, Dr. Charles Drayton . . . and there afterwards came Thomas Lynch, Paul Trapier, Thomas Heyward, Hugh Rutledge, Harris, Moultrie, Hume, Judge Grimke, Ralph Izard, Jr., Walter Izard, the Middletons and Stead."

It was an extraordinary group of young men who went to Westminster and Oxford. Not all studied at this famous old public school and university, however. William Bull of Ashley Hall plantation went to the University of Leyden in 1734, becoming the first native-born American to receive a medical degree. Gabriel Manigault, the planter-merchant, sent his son, Peter, abroad to study law at the Temple Bar and to travel extensively on the Continent. Henry Laurens, one of the city's wealthiest merchants, sent his sons to Switzerland and England to complete their studies.

Thus the young men of Charleston who were to direct a revolution and govern a new commonwealth were educated as English gentlemen. For a long time, in fact, English rule was sweet, and South Carolina enjoyed a golden age. But the young Charleston men who were received at the great houses of England's Whig families, who crowded the House of Commons gallery to hear Charles James Fox, Pitt, and Burke, were to learn that important posts in their home province were not for Carolinians but for English placemen. The injustice was keenly resented. One of the few colonials to attain a great place, Charles Pinckney, chief justice of the Province of South Carolina and father of the great Revolutionary leader, Charles Cotesworth Pinckney, had his job taken from him by an English political appointee. In this the rulers across the sea made a fatal error; the colonial ruling class developed a profound sense of grievance.

The Stamp Act agitation produced a change in the thinking of the Charleston men. It was a little thing, a stamp embossed on coarse, bluish paper, bearing the device of the English rose, crowned, and surmounted by the motto of the Garter, but it seemed to be a usurpation of colonial authority. There was great debate among the lawyers in the city, and in 1765 the Assembly appointed Thomas Lynch, John Rutledge, and Christopher Gadsden (whose grandson was to

negotiate the Gadsden Purchase) to attend the Stamp Act Congress in the North.

The same three men, with Henry Middleton and Edward Rutledge, were delegates to the First Continental Congress in 1774. The selection of an extremist like Gadsden to represent the Assembly was significant. This fiery Charlestonian had been educated in England, had served two years at sea aboard a British war vessel, and had returned to become a wealthy merchant and to become embroiled in a political controversy with the royal governor. Gadsden addressed mass meetings, wrote articles for the Charleston *Gazette,* and agitated unceasingly. At the First Continental Congress he expounded the view that separation from England was the only course to follow. Rutledge too was educated in England. He was a leader of the moderate faction in Charleston, opposing Gadsden's Separatist activities. When independence was proclaimed, however, Rutledge was given supreme power in South Carolina as president or "dictator" of the state. He was 37 years old.

War struck Charleston in full fury on June 28, 1776, when a British fleet attacked the hastily constructed palmetto-log fort on Sullivan's Island, commanding the mouth of the harbor. Local forces collected by Colonel William Moultrie repulsed the British, but the Carolinians suffered, nonetheless. British raiding parties, operating in the Charleston area during the years of the war, burned plantation houses, killed livestock, destroyed churches, carried off furniture and silver plate, and seized Negro slaves to be sold in the West Indies. Then another British squadron, under Lord Cornwallis and Sir Henry Clinton, descended upon Charleston in 1780. Against the advice of General Washington, the city resisted, but in vain, and on May 12 it was forced to surrender. The British took more than 5,400 Continental prisoners, together with all their ammunition and supplies. "The surrender was," a modern historian writes, "one of the greatest disasters suffered by the Americans during the whole war." Charleston remained under British rule for two and a half years.

In the postwar era the same families who had led the city in the Revolution still played a large role. Off to the North as representatives to the Constitutional Convention went John Rutledge, Charles Pinckney, Charles Cotesworth Pinckney, and Pierce Butler. Their work had large influence in giving a conservative hue to the document that emerged. Charles Pinckney, especially, had a profound understanding of statecraft; of the 84 provisions of the Constitution, at least 32 were taken from a draft he had made.

In appearance, at the end of the Revolution,

Charleston began to assert its independence of colonial styles. The heavy, squarish English house went out of fashion. In its place came the distinctive tall Charleston mansion of brick or cypress, with piazzas running the length of the building.

Captain Basil Hall, a visitor to Charleston after the war, wrote of "the villas of the wealthy planters, almost hid in the rich foliage," and of the "light oriental style of building, the gorgeous shrubs and flowers, and the tropical aspect of the city." It was in these years that Charlestonians turned to planting camellias, oleanders, jasmine, pomegranates, gardenias, fig trees—the floral elements associated with the city in after years.

Another postwar change was the development of the river rice plantation. By 1800 Low Country planters had learned how to harness the tides to do work for them, and rice culture moved from the inland swamps to the swamplands bordering the rivers along the coast. Enormous forests of cypress were felled, miles of dikes erected, and a complicated system of tidal gates constructed.

The successful clearing of the river swamps meant that more time for leisure was available to the leaders of this agrarian society. The new wealth and the new century brought a new zeal for style, elegance, and fine living, and a new spirit of aristocratic republicanism. The little oligarchy of rice and cotton planters who ruled Charleston found their pleasure at the dancing assemblies, the philharmonic concerts, the Jockey Ball, and innumerable dinners. Charlestonians relished nothing so much as an elegant dinner. Mrs. Ravenel described one dish that perhaps justifies that overworked adjective: it was called "a preserve of fowle," and the recipe began in this fashion: "Take all manner of Fowle and bone them all." The recipe then required that a small dove be put into a partridge; the partridge into a guinea hen; the guinea hen into a wild duck; the wild duck into a capon; the capon into a goose; the goose into a turkey or peacock.

Charleston's ruling oligarchy worshiped or did business in buildings designed by Robert Mills, one of the ablest architects in America; its members could discuss novels with William Gilmore Simms or poetry with Henry Timrod; they could have their portraits painted by Sully, Morse, or Jarvis—all of whom worked in Charleston—or miniatures painted by Charleston's own Charles Fraser; they could talk finances with Langdon Cheves, president of the Bank of the United States, or regional politics with Robert Barnwell Rhett, editor of the fire-eating *Charleston Mercury.*

The nineteenth-century planters, noted a French visitor, the Duc de Liancourt, were more European in outlook than the northern gentry. But there was more to it than a European outlook. Command over hundreds of slaves on isolated plantations, complete authority and responsibility, gave the planter class in the Low Country a supreme confidence in the rightness of their decisions, a boldness and independence that set them apart. There were many serious men among them, and the city was not always frivolous.

Politics, not business, was the chief interest of the men of Charleston in every period of its history. And there were versatile men, for example, Stephen Elliott, who in one lifetime managed to combine the careers of banker, botanist, planter, legislator, professor, and editor. Elliott was author of the first free-school bill in the South Carolina legislature, served for many years as president of the Bank of the State of South Carolina, shared in the establishment of what is today the Medical College of South Carolina and was its first professor of natural history, published a two-volume study on the botany of South Carolina and Georgia, managed his extensive plantation properties, and, in collaboration with Hugh Legaré, published the *Southern Review,* a quarterly of distinction.

Legaré served as a diplomat and was elected to Congress. He was attorney general of the United States in President Tyler's Cabinet and acting secretary of state at the time of his death in 1843. Legaré was a complete classical scholar; Parrington said of him that he had "the most cultivated mind in the South before the Civil War, and one of the most cultivated in America."

A somewhat similar figure was Joel R. Poinsett, a Charlestonian who was educated in New England and at Edinburgh, a linguist, a student of military science, and a world traveler who went into the remote regions of Russia and western Asia. In his long career Poinsett found time to act as a diplomatic observer for President Monroe; to be chief military advisor for a Chilean revolutionary army in a campaign against the Spanish; to be the first United States minister to Mexico; to serve in Congress and as secretary of war in President Van Buren's Administration; to serve his state as a legislator and director of a road-building project through the South Carolina mountains; and incidentally to collect the brilliant red blooms, the poinsettia, which have been named after him.

But the hero of Charleston was a man who was not even born there: John Caldwell Calhoun. Son of an upcountry pioneer, Calhoun was an aristocrat only in that he was an intellectual. It was Charleston, the city into which he had married, "whose rapt gaze was most fixed upon him as a demigod."

For the old city, he was the fulfillment of Lord Ashley's dream—the supremacy of natural excellence.

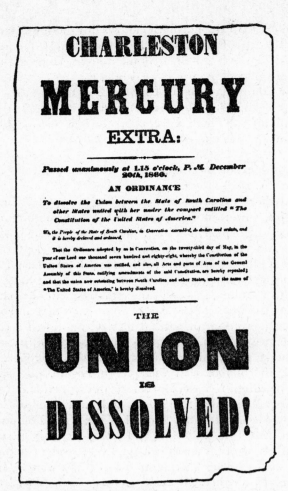

CHARLESTON
MERCURY
EXTRA:

Passed unanimously at 1.15 o'clock, P. M. December 20th, 1860.

AN ORDINANCE

To dissolve the Union between the State of South Carolina and other States united with her under the compact entitled " The Constitution of the United States of America."

We, the People of the State of South Carolina, in Convention assembled, do declare and ordain, and it is hereby declared and ordained,

That the Ordinance adopted by us in Convention, on the twenty-third day of May, in the year of our Lord one thousand seven hundred and eighty-eight, whereby the Constitution of the United States of America was ratified, and also, all Acts and parts of Acts of the General Assembly of this State, ratifying amendments of the said Constitution, are hereby repealed; and that the union now subsisting between South Carolina and other States, under the name of "The United States of America," is hereby dissolved.

THE
UNION
IS
DISSOLVED!

As this Charleston Mercury *clipping of December 20, 1860, indicates, South Carolina seceded by repealing its 1788 ratification of the Constitution. Four months later, with "every human being in Charleston" watching from the rooftops (opposite),* the Rebels fired on Sumter and war was on.

Calhoun, the tall, gaunt-faced "cast-iron man," led Charleston when, as one scholar has said, "Charleston ruled South Carolina, and South Carolina shaped Southern policy." He formulated the city's political and social philosophy. And it was the supreme achievement of Charleston to impart this philosophy to the Cotton South. While the North moved toward a broader democracy, Charleston, the spiritual center of an agrarian society, stressed the supremacy of excellence and rejected King Numbers.

Such was the strength of the ideal that Lord Ashley conceived and Calhoun developed that all the South, from Virginia to the Rio Grande, was ready to fight a war for it. Charleston was the force that could split the Union. Jeremiah Black, secretary of state in President Buchanan's Cabinet, acknowledged this power when he said to his assistant secretary, William Henry Trescott of South Carolina: "There, your little state,

no bigger than the palm of my hand, has broken up this mighty empire."

Charleston in 1860 was everything that aristocratic Lord Ashley might have desired. There was no other civilization like it in the United States. Five years later, Charleston, where the first shot was fired, arching over the bay toward Fort Sumter, went down under the tides of war. It fell to Federal troops as Sherman's forces swept along the Ashley River. The city itself was not bombarded; Sherman's troops simply made it militarily untenable by cutting its lines of communication and supply. In the process they destroyed almost every plantation in the area. Only Drayton Hall is still standing; and it would have been destroyed had not its owner turned it into a hospital.

"In our march through South Carolina," one of Sherman's soldiers recorded in his diary, "every man seemed to think that he had a free hand to burn any kind of property he could put the torch to. South Carolina paid the dearest penalty of any state in the Confederacy, considering the short time the Union army was in the state; and it was well that she should, for if South Carolina had not been so persistent in going to war, there would have been no war for years to come."

For Charleston, surrender was the beginning of the end. For in addition to the planters, a special breed of adventurous men, rice culture required a system of disciplined labor. When an alligator made a hole in a dike or a hurricane swept away a section of a bank, there had to be an available force of plantation workers to respond quickly and with skill to the instructions of the planter. With the end of slavery went the disciplined labor force. And the general disintegration of Charleston's economic life after 1865, combined with the successful introduction of highland rice in the Mississippi Valley and a series of disastrous hurricanes on the "Rice Coast," resulted in the ruin of Carolina's rice-planting industry by the end of the nineteenth century.

And so it was that Charleston, which had been third in per capita wealth in 1860, sank to the bottom. The beautiful shell remained and may be vastly enjoyed today, for poverty sealed the city against new building as effectively as the ashes did Pompeii. Northern democracy, industrial civilization, the force of numbers—they triumphed at last over the agrarian civilization of Lord Ashley and Calhoun.

Anthony Harrigan is editorial writer for The Charleston News and Courier *and a free-lance contributor to scholarly quarterlies and national magazines. His great-great-great-great-uncle, Richard Hutson, was the first Intendant (mayor) of Charleston after its incorporation in 1783.*

HARPER'S WEEKLY.
A JOURNAL OF CIVILIZATION.

Vol. V.—No. 227.]   NEW YORK, SATURDAY, MAY 4, 1861.   [SINGLE COPIES SIX CENTS.
[$2 50 PER YEAR IN ADVANCE.

Entered according to Act of Congress, in the Year 1861, by Harper & Brothers, in the Clerk's Office of the District Court for the Southern District of New York.

THE HOUSE-TOPS IN CHARLESTON DURING THE BOMBARDMENT OF SUMTER.

"The President came forward and
the sun burst through the clouds"

CONTINUED FROM PAGE 15

"Stanton and Seward retired to the left at some distance from the President and sat down together. They seemed very friendly. Stanton had his arm around Seward's neck and constantly whispered in his ear. Welles sat by himself, and Justice Chase sat erect and dignified, evidently reflecting that he ought to be in Lincoln's place. Senator Sumner stood prominently forward as if to attract attention. . . . The President smiled to himself and seemed greatly to enjoy the sunshine which now streamed upon him. He was dressed in black, with a plain frock coat. In his hand he held a printed copy of his inaugural address. The marshals of the day were grouped around the President, swelling with pride, and often excluding him from sight. The planks of the platform were wet, and the airy position rather chilly. The bands played away most lustily, and their 'Hail to the Chief' could scarcely be stopped.

"From the platform nothing could be seen but a sea of faces below and a sea of mud beyond. . . . In the Capitol all the windows were filled with ladies, and the steps and esplanade at the north wing presented the same dense crowd that the central steps did, while on the unfinished parts of the south wing, on all the scaffolding, hundreds of soldiers had clambered up and decorated all that part with the army blue. . . . As the President came forward there was a cheer but not a great one, and at the same time the sun burst through the clouds, and, though pretty well to the south, lighted up the whole east face very brilliantly. . . .

"At about one o'clock . . . the President rose and stepped forward to the reading desk. He was greeted with very faint applause; indeed there was no enthusiasm throughout the address. It was not strictly an inaugural address, since it was read before Mr. Lincoln took the oath. It was more like a valedictory. The President read in a very loud, clear voice, and hundreds of the audience could hear it.

"During the delivery of the speech Stanton and Seward were remarkably attentive, rising and bending forward to listen. The crowd kept pushing nearer and nearer the platform. Sumner smiled superciliously at the frequent scriptural quotations. Negroes ejaculated 'Bress de Lord' in a low murmur at the end of almost every sentence. Beyond this there was no cheering of any consequence. . . . After a brief pause the President and Chief Justice rose together and the oath of office was administered. The voice of the Chief Justice was inaudible, but the workings of his countenance could be distinctly seen as he labored to be impressive. Then there was a cheer, and the President came forward and bowed and smiled. During the whole ceremony he looked unusually handsome. When delivering his speech his face glowed with enthusiasm, and he evidently felt every word that he uttered.

"Cries for Andy Johnson next ensued. There was a momentary delay and then the Vice President presented himself and waved both hands. There were calls of 'Speech! Speech!' and some applause when Andy appeared. He rubbed his red face with his hands as if to clear up his ideas, but did not succeed and said nothing. A lane was then opened through the crowd on the platform, and the presidential party retired into the Capitol amid the thunders of artillery in Capitol Square and the music of the bands."

One incident that went almost unnoticed had to do with the strange actions of a man who had a card of admission to the Capitol which he had probably procured through Senator John P. Hale of New Hampshire, for he was secretly engaged to marry the Senator's daughter. This good-looking young man tried to force his way through the line of police as the President passed. He was forcibly ejected from the rotunda, but, oddly enough, was not arrested. Weeks later, when the nation-wide man hunt for the President's assassin was under way, a photograph of this man was shown to Benjamin B. French, commissioner of public buildings, who had been present when the intruder behaved so oddly. He identified the picture as a portrait of John Wilkes Booth, the celebrated actor of an even more celebrated theatrical family. And one of Booth's friends testified that the violently pro-Southern actor had said: "What an excellent chance I had to kill the President, if I had wished, on inauguration day!"

Unaware of the presence in the Capitol of the man who was destined to slay him just 41 days later, Abraham Lincoln, now inaugurated as President of the United States for the second time, was led to his waiting carriage to return to the White House. As the President's carriage was about to leave, his eleven-year-old son, little Tad, scrambled into it. Mrs. Lincoln and their first-born son, Robert Todd Lincoln, who had just been made a captain on Grant's staff, followed in other carriages.

Walt Whitman wrote about Lincoln's return to the White House: "He was in his plain two-horse barouche, and looked very much worn and tired; the lines, indeed, of vast responsibilities, intricate questions, and demands of life and death, cut deeper than ever upon his dark brown face; yet all the goodness, tenderness, sadness, and canny shrewdness [showed] underneath the furrows."

And so ended one of the most memorable inaugurations in American history. The senators re-entered the Senate chamber, paying little attention to the President's speech but discussing Johnson's behavior with the petty spite of washerwomen gossiping over a back yard fence. They waited for the new Vice President to appear, so he could officially adjourn the Senate, but he never came and thus brought more malicious comment down upon himself. Finally the senators departed by ones and twos, and the great halls of the Capitol became silent.

Lincoln is sometimes thought of as having been too lenient and easygoing, but he could be firm when the situation required strength and decisiveness. The next-to-last sentence of the address he delivered that day shows how determined he was to finish the stern task to which he was committed. But the unyielding attitude of the Old Testament changes quickly in the famous peroration, which is much nearer to the New Testament in thought and words:

. . . Fondly do we hope—fervently do we pray—that this mighty scourge of war may speedily pass away. Yet, if God wills that it continue until all the wealth piled by the bondsman's two hundred and fifty years of unrequited toil shall be sunk, and until every drop of blood drawn with the lash shall be paid by another drawn with the sword, as was said three thousand years ago, so still it must be said, "The judgments of the Lord are true and righteous altogether."

With malice toward none; with charity for all; with firmness in the right, as God gives us to see the right, let us strive on to finish the work we are in; to bind up the nation's wounds; to care for him who shall have borne the battle and for his widow, and his orphan—to do all which may achieve and cherish a just and a lasting peace among ourselves, and with all nations.

The President's arduous day was not yet over. He had to greet several thousand people at a White House levee that evening. It was still an American tradition that anyone could attend such a public reception who had the patience and the strength to wait for hours to gain admission. It was also a tradition that the President must stand in the receiving line to shake each person's hand and utter a few meaningless words of greeting.

After dinner Cabinet members and their families began arriving early at the White House in order to have a few moments with the President before the crowd got in. A temporary wooden platform had been erected at one of the East Room windows so the long line of visitors could be channeled past the President, across the room, and then out through the high window to the side street. At eight o'clock, when the gates were thrown open, some two thousand people tried to storm the main entrance. The doors to the White House were opened for only a few minutes at a time in order to control the rate of entry. Even with this precaution the *Chronicle* reported that "some of the more unfortunate females, who were caught in the surging mass, actually shrieked with pain while several fainted and were carried away."

When the visitors got inside they were hurried through the halls to the East Room, where the Marine Band was playing and where government and military dignitaries were clustered in exclusive little groups around the formal reception room. There, according to the *Star*, "The President, in a plain black suit with white kid gloves, was in excellent spirits . . . and received all visitors cordially. It is estimated that he shook hands with between five and six thousand persons during the course of the evening. Mrs. Lincoln was also kept fully occupied. . . . She was dressed most charmingly in an elegant white satin dress, the skirt tastefully draped with black lace, a rich black lace shawl . . . a costly pearl necklace, etc., etc."

The carpets were covered to protect them from mud brought in on the visitors' feet, and soldiers and police guided the line of eager people through the hallways. But despite these precautions, the visitors did some damage, as they always did when they were permitted to invade the White House. Even the watchful soldiers and Metropolitan Police could not entirely prevent the souvenir hunting and actual vandalism that were characteristic of American sightseers in the mid-nineteenth century. William H. Crook, one of the President's bodyguards, said that "a great piece of red brocade, a yard square almost, was cut from the window-hangings of the East Room, and another piece, not quite so large, from a curtain in the Green Room. Besides this, flowers from the floral design in the lace curtains were cut out, evidently for an ornament for the top of pincushions or something of the sort."

The crush went on all evening. Those who came by carriage had to wait for several hours while the long line of vehicles slowly unloaded passengers. At eleven o'clock a large crowd was still trying to gain admission, but the doors were firmly closed on the hour, and the latecomers had to go home without seeing the President. Just before midnight the Marine Band played "Yankee Doodle," and the White House was then cleared of guests so rapidly that the downstairs rooms were dark before the clock struck twelve.

At noon on Monday, March 6, the Senate, sitting in extra session, was called to order by the new Vice President. As soon as the formalities of the day were over, Henry Wilson of Massachusetts got up to ask for the floor. When Vice President Johnson recognized him and gave him the right to speak, he proposed a resolution that was intended to be a deliberate insult to the Senate's new leader. It directed "the sergeant-at-arms to remove from the Senate side of the Capitol the sale of intoxicating or spirituous liquors." Wilson said that he was willing to let his resolution lie over until the next day, but his colleague from Massachusetts, Charles Sumner, got up to ask very coolly, "Why not act upon it now?" Everyone must have felt very uncomfortable, but no one dared to offer an objection so the resolution was considered passed. The sergeant-at-arms promptly closed the bar known as "The Hole in the Wall," and the sign over it which read EXCLUSIVELY FOR SENATORS was turned to the wall.

The great Inauguration Ball was held in the Patent Office that evening. The north wing had just been completed, and the building formed an enormous quadrangle, with an open court in the center. Part of the building's spacious halls had served as a military hospital from October, 1861, to March, 1863.

All four of the enormous second-story rooms, each one approximately 270 feet long and 60 feet wide, were used for the ball. The south wing, with its elaborate and colorful English tiled floor, tall pillars, and large glass showcases, was the main entrance. The east wing was used as a promenade leading to the north wing, which was to be the main ballroom. The elaborate supper was served in the west wing at midnight.

The engraved tickets cost ten dollars each; the price entitled a gentleman to bring as many ladies as he wished. The local newspaper had made it clear that—contrary to rumor—Negroes would not be admitted to the ballroom, although many of them were, of course, employed as waiters and servants. Three orchestras were used; the one that provided the dance music was conducted by Professor William Withers, Jr., leader of the orchestra at Ford's Theatre.

The north hall was described by the Washington *Morning Chronicle* as being "magnificently decorated with our glorious national emblem, large banners being festooned from the ceiling to the floor. Between the windows were artistically disposed guidons and

corps insignia, bearing the marks of the various army corps, brigades, and regiments of the United States service, while miniature American flags were crossed and placed at intervals on the walls. Over the main entrance approaching from the east, on a balcony, was stationed a fine military band, and midway in the hall, on the southern side, upon another balcony, tastefully decorated, as was the former, with bunting, was placed the orchestra under the care of Mr. Withers. So, between the two bands, the music . . . was kept up constantly. On a raised dais immediately opposite the latter balcony, and on the northern side of the hall, were placed handsome sofas of blue and gold adornment . . . as seats of honor for the President and his suite." The New York *World* was unhappy about the dais and its gold chairs, muttering editorially that "it needed but little imagination to transform them into thrones."

The first guests arrived shortly before nine o'clock and were sent down the long dirty halls where puddles of water had been left by hurrying waiters and where department clerks still sat with feet propped up on their desks, puffing vigorously on their cigars while they inspected the pretty girls in their colorful evening dresses. People kept coming until midnight, by which time some four thousand guests had arrived. The party began at ten, when the military band in the north hall played a National Inauguration March that had been especially composed for the occasion; after this a grand promenade around the ballroom was staged with much ceremony. Quadrilles, lancers, schottisches, polkas, and waltzes then followed. The New York *World* had a poor opinion of the crowd and the dancing, saying that "the men threw their legs around like the spokes of a wheel; the women hopped, skipped and jumped about in a manner which would have made a French dancing master commit suicide. They appeared to think that every other dance was a waltz and acted accordingly and exhibited the greatest science when they were kicking up the most dust."

About half-past ten there was a sudden pause, the military band took over and struck up "Hail to the Chief," while a passageway was formed through the crowd for the entrance of the presidential party. The President came down the aisle with Schuyler Colfax, followed by Mrs. Lincoln, who was escorted by Senator Charles Sumner. The *Chronicle* said that "the procession promenaded the entire length of the hall. . . . Mrs. Lincoln was attired in faultless taste. She wore a white silk skirt, a bertha of point lace and puffs of silk, and a white fan, trimmed with ermine and silvered spangles, white kid gloves and lace handkerchief, and a necklace, bracelet, and earrings of pearls. Her hair was brushed closely back from her forehead, and a head-dress, composed of a wreath of white jessamines [sic] and purple violets, with long trailing vines, completed a most *recherché* costume. The President was dressed in a full suit of black, with white kid gloves."

Later in the evening members of the Cabinet and the diplomatic corps made their entry. Vice President Johnson was apparently well enough to attend, and his appearance, after his rebuff in the Senate that day, started tongues to wagging. The crowd pressed in close around the central platform to stare at the President and the other celebrities there. Among the notables on the platform was Captain Robert Todd Lincoln in full-dress uniform, paying close attention to the daughter of the senator from Iowa, Mary Eunice Harlan, whom he was later to marry.

Much of the gossip during the evening centered around the Lincoln family. Little Tad's imperious manner in dealing with the Black Horse Cavalry, which had been detailed to guard the White House, was a favorite topic of discussion. "Are we to have a Prince Imperial?" the New York *Herald* asked querulously.

The appointment of Tad's older brother, Robert Lincoln, as a captain on Grant's staff had come in for some criticism, but now that he was at last in the army, the public had lost much of its hostility toward him. Mrs. Lincoln, however, had many real enemies. Her relatives in the Confederacy, her extravagance in costume, and her expenditures for decorating the White House in wartime made her unpopular.

The President and his party were shown into the supper room first and were seated at the head of a 250-foot-long table so they could eat in peace before the crowd was admitted. They thus had a chance to see the display in all its gastronomic glory. The center ornament was a huge model of the Capitol made of pastry covered with white icing. This stood on a large pedestal upon which were other pastry models, including one of Fort Sumter with realistic-looking ironclads around it; a group of Washington and his generals; a symbolic statue of Liberty; as well as such abstract ideas as "The Progress of Civilization" and "The Advance of the Arts and Sciences in America."

The cooks had been working busily to get the great feast ready. The elaborate bill of fare included fish, beef, veal, game, poultry, and smoked meats, each prepared in a variety of ways; chicken and lobster salads; eight confections called "ornamental pyramides" and a dozen kinds of cakes and tarts; ice cream in six flavors and ices in three; coffee and chocolate.

It was fortunate that the presidential party was permitted to begin eating before the crowd was admitted to the supper room. As soon as the doors were opened, there was a general rush. According to the *Star*, "The onset of the crowd upon the tables was frightful, and nothing but the immense reserves of eatables would have supplied the demand, or rather the waste. Numbers . . . with more audacity than good taste, could be seen snatching whole *pâtés*, chickens, legs of veal, halves of turkeys, ornamental pyramids, &s., from the tables, and bearing them aloft over the heads of the shuddering crowd, (ladies especially, with greasy ruin to their dresses impending) . . .

"The floor of the supper room was soon sticky, pasty and oily with wasted confections, mashed cakes and debris of fowl and meat. The . . . appropriaters of eatables from the tables left their plates upon the floor . . . adding to the difficulty of locomotion; and gentlemen, in conscientiously giving a wide berth to a lady's skirt, not infrequently steered clear of Scylla only to fall upon a Charybdis of greasy crockery. Finally everybody was satisfied, even those who felt bound to 'eat their ten dollars' worth' . . . the ball room again filled up, and the dance . . . was resumed."

When the President and his party wanted to leave, they found it impossible to pass through the mob that was still raiding the food tables. They had to enter an alcove between display cases and then go upstairs to a balcony from which they could make their way through devious and little-used narrow passages to an obscure side exit. No one paid any attention to them as they went, for the guests were so busy getting food, eating it, or chattering while they waited for someone to bring it, that they did not care about anything else.

The grand ball went on until the early morning hours, and the sky was beginning to lighten when the party finally broke up. When the last reveler left the Patent Office that morning and daylight came in through the high windows to reveal the unpleasant mess which was all that remained of the once-imposing display that had been set out on the supper tables, President Lincoln's second term had been officially and socially launched.

Philip Van Doren Stern, a student of Lincoln and the Civil War, has contributed several articles to AMERICAN HERITAGE. *This article is adapted from* An End to Valor, *soon to be published by Houghton Mifflin Co.*

Thirty feet over the Farmington River

The Farmington Canal

Written and illustrated by ERIC SLOANE

The first years of the 1800's in America were loud with canal talk. The enormous success of the Erie Canal had aroused engineering instincts in every American. Even the barnyard was invaded; inventive farmers were building small canals from their farms to the nearest river, some had devised sluiceways from barn to barn for floating heavy loads instead of hauling them in wagons, and others made canal ways from their land to the nearest mill to float logs and grain boats instead of braving the yard-thick mud of the roads. The wheel seemed doomed to obsolescence. Oxcart hauling was two-mile-an-hour transportation limited to good weather; a level highway usable in every weather seemed the answer to all travel.

The canal era was the first American school of engineering; only after the Erie Canal did civil engineering become a recognized profession. The great names of early American engineering were largely those of men who had served apprenticeship on the Erie project; but the men who gouged the countryside with a maze of smaller canals are forgotten. Long before excavating machines were devised, men were digging hundred-mile canals through mountainous country with nothing but picks and shovels. The

vast extent of such hand labor is almost beyond conception.

One canal, dug by hand shovel through the rocky New England hills, is a classic example, for it embodies the spirit of the canal era at the very moment when America turned to railroads and sounded the era's knell. The Farmington Canal line stretched from New Haven on Long Island Sound, through the middle of Connecticut, and into the center of Massachusetts—a distance of over eighty miles. To tell the average Yankee of today that hand shovels once built a waterway to float huge boats through New England all but exhausts his credulity. The Farmington has long since vanished into the landscape, transformed into roadbeds for railroads and automobile highways. Many towns that were built along its banks are nowadays unaware that it ever existed. But though the full story of American canals is too complex or obscure to be recorded fully, antiquarians like those who "collect" covered bridges are now delving into canal history, identifying thousands of ditches—their strange stone abutments overgrown with alders—that dot the back country.

It was in 1822, at a meeting in Farmington, Connecticut, that New Englanders began to speak of equaling the Erie Canal with a waterway from Long Island Sound to Canada. The project would run directly through New England, making the region the center of commerce of all America. The same year a charter was granted, and the Farmington Canal Company began getting estimates on quantity orders for shovels and wheelbarrows. The year after, a survey had been completed and an estimate made of the cost of the canal through Connecticut: $420,698.88. The Mechanics Bank of New Haven was chartered on condition of its subscribing $200,000 of the canal company's stock, and after another year the necessary money had been raised. On July 4, 1825, a ceremony was set for Granby, near the Massachusetts line, where excavation was to commence.

July 4 fell on a Monday that year, but the preparations were so great that spontaneous celebrations broke out on the day before, and accusations by the clergy who had gathered for the occasion led to prophecies of doom because of the Sabbath-breaking. Another evil omen occurred when the gilt shovel with which Governor Oliver Wolcott was turning the first spadeful of earth broke in half. The cautious Yankees were doubtful about the canal from the beginning, and every event seemed to hint of failure. But the celebra-

tion was the biggest that New England had ever seen: three thousand people were in attendance, the Simsbury artillery performed, and a canalboat on wheels drawn by six horses came all the way from New Haven with Captain George Rowland aboard. A procession two miles long followed, and a supper was served on the green.

After two years, the little hole begun by Governor Wolcott had deepened into a ditch 36 feet wide from the Massachusetts line to the waters of the Sound. The heaviest machine that had been used was a horse scoop no bigger than the one any farmer kept in his barn. The tools were picks, shovels, and wheelbarrows.

During the building of the canal, the whole state of Connecticut boomed. Taverns were built along the banks, and land was sold as being "close to the canal." Industries grew beside the ditch even before it held water.

"On June 20, 1828," Deacon Hooker recorded, "a multitude of people collected to witness the launching and sailing of the first canalboat seen in Farmington." The Deacon went on to say that "bell-ringing, cannon-firing and music by the Phoenix Band were accompaniments. The boat (named James Hillhouse) was drawn by four large gray horses handsomely decked

July 4th 1825 at Granby, Connecticut

Cross-roads in the Canal days

and rode by as many black boys dressed in white." It was launched and the canal was at last in use.

From 1828 till 1835, when construction was completed to the Connecticut River at Northampton, Massachusetts, the canal enjoyed a period of romantic activity. Pleasure excursions were the canal's specialty, but wood products, cider, maple sugar, and meal actually floated down its surface from the north, while salt, oysters, rum, coal, and hardware sailed back into the New England hills. Itinerant vendors with floating stores wandered along the route, underselling the shops ashore and incurring frowns and even hostile ordinances from canalside towns. Yankee peddlers abandoned their well-known wagons and built scows festooned with flags and advertisements. Some were small enough to be poled by hand rather than drawn by horses. Citizens attended town meetings, did their shopping, and even went to church by boat.

But the picture was not all rosy. To begin with, farmers were most unfriendly to a project which had cut their lands in two and drained their bog meadows. Planned "disasters" occurred almost daily: embankments were dug away, tributary streams blocked, and bridges toppled over. One farmer who had a grudge against a neighbor made a break in the canal bank and flooded his antagonist's farm. Lawsuits took up more of the canal officials' time than anything else. In the second place, droughts and floods were unkindly toward the Farmington; in 1843 floods damaged it and the whole fall trade was lost; 1845 saw it close down for lack of water. And finally, repairs and maintenance were costing more than tolls—the canal's only source of revenue—brought in; by 1846 the stockholders had refused to make further advances. The canal had yielded $75,000 a year in its best times, yet overall it had shown the staggering loss of $1,377,156.54.

Then, in 1847, a railroad opened to Plainville, and in that same year a break in the canal caused a barge full of coal to be swept out into the river and overturned. Public sentiment turned away from the canal and concentrated upon the railroad. Almost overnight the canal ceased to be. Taverns became dwellings, farmers moved in and blocked up portions of the canal for their own use, muskrats and rushes took over the banks, and small boys commandeered unused stretches for fishing places. The Farmington Canal was dead.

It was not, however, a complete loss. It opened a shorter route through the middle of New England and prepared a level roadbed for railroad travel. It stimulated business in regions which might otherwise still be back-country farms today, and it sparked the Yankee imagination. One of the Farmington's little-known claims to fame, for example, was an early propeller-driven canalboat. Connecticut inventor Benjamin Beecher designed it a few years before Ericsson's propeller had been perfected. He built his boat in an abandoned sawmill, taking it to Cheshire during the winter on an ox-drawn sled and launching it in a frozen creek.

Beecher's boat was run by a steam engine he had designed himself; from the prow extended his "water-gimlet," a reverse-action propeller which pulled the boat instead of pushing it. On her first trip the craft carried a group of financial backers four miles upstream and back, but the speed was disappointing. Not only was she slower than paddle-wheel boats, she could be beaten even by horse-pulled barges. A later trip, designed to interest the same group in financing changes in the propeller, ended in engine failure. The passengers had to walk back, and the boat was beached indefinitely. Long after the canal was abandoned, she lay on her side near Cheshire Center, like a monument to the inventiveness and hopelessness of the great ditch itself.

Eric Sloane, an expert on early Americana and a frequent contributor to AMERICAN HERITAGE, *lives in New Milford, Connecticut.*

Benjamin Beecher's Propeller

Unwanted Treasures
of the Patent Office

CONTINUED FROM PAGE 19

propriation, and still new ones poured in. Finally the law had to be changed again, this time to *prohibit* the sending of a model unless demanded by the Patent Commissioner.

But still no record was made of how many models had been restored or even how many were in the Patent Office, and estimates varied by as many as 25,000, depending on whether the guesser was a patent examiner tripping over them while trying to do a day's work or a congressman looking to save the price of renting some place to put them. It is known, however, that 246,094 patents had been issued by 1880 and that perhaps 200,000 of them were represented by models. Added to these were thousands of models which had accompanied applications that were never completed.

By 1893 the Patent Office estimate appears to have won out, for that year Congress allowed the renting of the Union Building at G Street between Sixth and Seventh streets, N.W. No attempt was made to arrange the models for display in the Union Building. They were simply stored in fantastic disarray throughout the building, even though Congress was under the impression it was paying for an exhibition hall.

This folly was not discovered until 1907, when the owners of the Union Building attempted to raise the rent and thus precipitated a congressional investigation. The annual number of visitors, it came out, was none. In retaliation, without thought as to why there were no visitors, Congress in 1908 decided to sell all the models, first giving the Smithsonian Institution six months to pick out those it wanted. The Smithsonian managed to find only 1,061 worth keeping. At a public auction, 3,000 models of inventions that had failed to receive patents were sold for $62.18.

During the next two decades those remaining unsold, amounting to 155,939, were carted about repeatedly—back to the Patent Office, to a leaky basement under the House of Representatives, to the basement of the District of Columbia's Male Work House, and at last to an abandoned livery stable. Finally, in a congressional economy wave in 1925, it was found that more than $200,000 had been spent for storage and moving since 1884; rather than squander any more money on museums, Congress again elected to sell. An act was passed on February 13, 1925, appropriating $10,000 for the sale and creating a three-member commission to again select important models for the Smith-

sonian and other recognized museums.

By late November, the Smithsonian had selected about 2,500, and 2,600 more were taken either by other museums or by inventors. Another 50,000, which had been unpacked, so crammed the floor space that an immediate auction was ordered, and on December 3, 1925, they went for $1,550. Thomas E. Robertson, patent commissioner, reported to Congress that "this was thought to be a good figure."

The buyer of the 50,000 models was never officially identified; the General Supply Committee kept scanty records. Circumstances, however, point to Sir Henry Wellcome, who in 1926 came back to acquire the remaining 125,000, cases and all, unopened, without even the formality of a public auction. He paid $6,540.

Sir Henry began life in Wisconsin in frontier days—his earliest memories were of holding the basin while his doctor-uncle dressed the wounds of pioneers who had been battling Indians—but he had become a British subject during World War I. He founded Burroughs, Wellcome & Co., a large and successful drug house, and was knighted by George V for his services to medicine and pharmaceutics. Given to offbeat causes (he once endowed a trust to provide translations of textbooks for Chinese medical students), Sir Henry decided to start a patent-model museum and to store his new acquisitions at the Burroughs, Wellcome plant in Tuckahoe, New York, until he could get around to building it.

When Sir Henry died ten years later, at the age of 82, the models were still there, packed in their original cases, unopened. The trustees of his estate, after lengthy consideration of what to do with them, finally decided to sell. It took them two years, but they got their price—$50,000.

Their customer was Crosby Gaige, Broadway producer and gourmet, whose collections to date had been limited to books on eating and cooking and to laboratory equipment for making his own tooth paste.

Gaige brought the models to Rockefeller Center with the kind of fanfare usually reserved for the circus. Without delay he cracked open the first few cases. Then, on August 8, 1938, he managed to entice several representatives of the press into being present while an expert locksmith twirled the dial of a model crystallized-iron safe.

The tumblers clicked; the door swung open. Inside was a paper. The writing was faint, but the signature was legible—A. Lincoln. The paper was a petition for a patent on a flatboat with air chambers for floating it over shoals, invented by Lincoln in 1849. Flash bulbs popped and the models were page one news.

Within a few more days, Gaige plucked from the cases the original model of the Gatling gun, the first dentist's chair, and the first egg beater (Timothy Earle, 1866). He also had a long list of bedazzled customers, and by early October, 1938, he and his silent partner, Douglas G. Hertz (fight manager, movie actor, mule trader, survivor of the *Lusitania,* and former owner of the New York Yankees football team), had retired with a neat profit from speculation in Americana by selling out to a group of businessmen for $75,000. The Lincoln paper, its purpose served, disappeared as mysteriously as it had arrived.

The new owners also had money-making ideas but lacked Gaige's theatrical imagination. They incorporated under the name of American Patent Models and unpacked 25,000 models, a tiny part of the collection, amid mutterings to the press that it was an outrage the government had ever sold them. The vast remainder, about 2,600 full cases, was shipped to the Neptune Storage Warehouse in New Rochelle, New York. Some 500 of the unpacked models were then fitted into special crates and sent out in three separate caravans across the country, to be displayed in department stores and other showrooms for a fee. The rest were kept at Rockefeller Center.

Between 1939 and 1941 the models, uncatalogued, unclassified, and on public display, proved to be no more of an attraction than they had been years before. Neptune Storage filed a lien of $7,954 for warehousing the unopened crates. Rockefeller Center wanted its rent. American Patent Models, in a desperate effort to raise money, reduced prices on all models to $1 each and for quick cash sold a collection of Civil War ordnance to an unnamed buyer. An unlisted number of other models went in the same manner. Then came bankruptcy. In 1942 a court ordered the company dissolved and the models auctioned for whatever they would fetch over and above Neptune's bill (which had grown to $10,814) and another $800 to warehouses in Minneapolis, Salt Lake City, and Oakland, California, where the traveling exhibits were stranded.

At this point O. Rundle Gilbert, an auctioneer, learned of the models. Gilbert brought in several partners and shortly, in exchange for $2,100 plus the storage charges, they were the owners of about 200,000 patent models. Seventy-five huge trailer truckloads later, the models were in Gilbert's barns at Garrison, New York, but their adventures were far from finished. Gilbert's partners, eager for profit, insisted on a new auction, and when more than 3,000 persons came to see a display of 2,000 models which opened at the Architectural League in New York City on April 14, 1943, they were confident of success. But despite great spectator interest only three actual bidders showed up on the day of the sale. Among them they bought 400

models. Back to Garrison went the remaining 1,600; the round trip, display, and other costs had exceeded the gross by $3,000.

Gilbert then began systematic unpacking. Soon, with the help of his wife and three hired hands, Gilbert was delving into boxes which presumably had not been opened since 1908 and which the Smithsonian Commission of 1925 had not had a chance to examine.

Slowly, as the models were unpacked, identified, and classified—for the Gilberts believed they would sell best in groups describing the complete development of a particular item—they were moved into a stucco house on the estate, where they filled fourteen rooms. The rest of the house was rented to a young couple and their children.

Identification was easy in the case of models which bore labels; some of them were stamped with dates prior to 1836 and evidently were among those reconstructed after the fire of that year. But many of the models were without any identification at all and these were set aside for further research.

One group of models, including farm equipment and an early baseball mask, was sold to the Farmer's Museum and the Baseball Museum at Cooperstown, New York. By Spring, 1945, several other groups, including one which traced the entire history of the sewing machine, were also ready for sale. There were perhaps 20,000 models in the stucco house at Garrison— close to 3,000 of them various forms of bolts and nuts— when fire broke out. The young couple and their children were saved, but nothing else.

Stunned, the Gilberts decided to leave the remaining 2,000 unopened cases in the barns until they felt better. Then, some four years later, the idea of a museum of their own began to intrigue them. As a start they purchased a vast barn in Center Sandwich, New Hampshire, and moved in about 1,000 models chosen at random. They started charging 25 cents, 50 cents, then $1, and found that, no matter what the price, Center Sandwich was good for 75 visitors a day. They also found that sometimes people who stopped could help them decide what some of the objects were. One man told them they had the model of the first rotary press; another found the first Mergenthaler typesetting machine, which he promptly took apart but never returned to put back together again.

Others guessed that some of the models, with their fine tooling and hand workmanship, must have cost more than $1,000 to make. When word of this reached Gilbert's partners in 1950, the pressure was on again for another sale.

This time the idea was to invade Gimbels, a proposition which the department store welcomed with open arms. "Gimbels is nuts over patent models. You'll be nuts over them too," cried their advertisements.

Hastily, without time for classification, the Gilberts ripped open 200 or 300 more cases in the Garrison barns and shipped the contents to Gimbels in New York and Philadelphia. Among them were the "Bretzel bending machine" invented by a Mr. Bretzel, who formed his crackers in the shape of a B (the public quickly decided a pretzel was easier to pronounce), and such novelties as a hen house which, when the chicken went out for scratching, dropped down a sign saying, "I am out. You may have my egg." There were also an 1825 plug of navy chewing tobacco and an 1869 parlor bathtub. In one lot was some powdered milk patented in 1863; Mr. Gilbert added water, tasted it, and pronounced it "sweet as ever." The prices ran from $1 to $1,000, the latter tag attached to the Gatling gun.

Again there were thousands of spectators but few buyers, with the exception of Gilbert, who took advantage of his partners' disappointment to buy them out at cost. He shipped the 5,000 or so models which had been stranded at the two Gimbels stores (about 600 had been sold) to his museum at Center Sandwich,

where they remained until 1952, when he purchased as a new museum an abandoned hospital at Plymouth, New Hampshire, and moved the entire display there. But in his barns at Garrison, still unopened, unseen since 1908, there are cases which contain anywhere from 100,000 to 120,000 more models.

Gilbert calculates that with the new museum he has put well over $85,000 into the models since acquiring them fifteen years ago, and he does not intend to invest any more. Those that are still packed will stay that way until he sees a good reason to open them. Sometimes he wishes the government would buy the collection back and put it someplace—Ellis Island, for instance. In the meantime he operates the Plymouth museum every summer. And when he and Mrs. Gilbert are at their home in Garrison, they occasionally go over to the barns and look at those rows on rows of boxes.

Donald W. Hogan is assistant city editor of the New York Herald Tribune. *A free-lance writer whose major interest is American history, he has contributed articles to several national magazines.*

"... *Especially pretty Alice*" CONTINUED FROM PAGE 64

off, one morning, in a jaunting car from Killarney. For a guide they had "a very nice old Irishman" who took them through the Gap of Dunlo and watched with Celtic melancholy their reaction to the Black Valley; "as dreary a place as I ever saw," Theodore wrote, "because of the black mist which rose from the peat bogs." Ireland was a beautiful country, but with an "under-stratum of wretchedness." Roosevelt had seen, probably for the first time in his life, actual hunger. They had run into a man on the Cork road who was weak from starvation and had helped him out with a shilling or two. It had been a depressing ending to the day.

Summer found them in Switzerland, where Theodore had a chance to demonstrate his physical fitness still further by some mountain climbing. Alice was, of course, left behind, for in those days women rarely joined in such strenuous diversions. Her husband seems to have agreed with the current attitude; at least he does not mention missing Alice's company or express regret that she had not shared with him the majesty of the mountain peaks.

They continued without hurrying and made no attempt to emulate tourists anxious to see all of Europe in thirty days. By August they had been down the Rhine, and Roosevelt wrote to his sister that work on

his book had suffered during their travels. He was, in fact, undergoing the discouragements that are the lot of authors. He was, characteristically, wondering whether his inability to get *The Naval War of 1812* written did not signify that he was to be a failure in other things. "I have plenty of information," he complained, "but I can't get it into words; I wonder if I won't find everything in life too big for my abilities. Well, time will tell." Fortunately for the progress of this pedantic history, Alice and Theodore spent some weeks with the Bulloch family at Liverpool. There Roosevelt had long conferences with the uncle who had been a captain in the Confederate Navy. Nautical mysteries were clarified. The book went on.

Before crossing the Channel, they had stopped in Paris, where Alice had done the inevitable shopping, and where they had looked at Napoleon's tomb. No longer was Theodore bored, as he had been eleven years before. His interest in war, in manly prowess, had grown. This time he experienced "a solemn feeling" in looking at the bier of "the mightiest conqueror the world ever saw." Then, in revulsion, he added: "... otherwise, I suppose, [he] was an almost unmixed evil."

They returned home toward the end of September, with Theodore expecting to continue his law studies.

But within a few weeks he found himself the candidate of his party for election to the state legislature. He was soon making stump speeches while his friends alternated between amusement and indignation that a young man of good blood, with opportunity for a legal career before him, should stoop to the gutter of American politics. Alice and Theodore were still making their home with Mrs. Roosevelt, but after Election Day they prepared to move to Albany. He was now the Honorable Theodore Roosevelt, assemblyman-elect from the Twenty-first District.

Here, the story of Alice Lee becomes increasingly unsubstantial. It is known that during his first year at Albany, beginning in January, 1882, Roosevelt took rooms in a quasi hotel where fellow legislators stayed. It is known that Alice was there with him the first winter and also that they returned to New York for most of their week ends. Isaac L. Hunt, an assemblyman from the northern part of the state, remembered her as "a very charming woman, tall and willowy. I was very much taken with her." On the whole, Alice must have been decidedly bored. She had little, if any, interest in politics. There must have been periods that dragged interminably. Then, in the summer of 1883, she knew that she was to have a baby, and Roosevelt, if his subsequent enthusiasm for quantity production of offspring is any indication, was delighted. Meanwhile, they had taken a house at No. 55 West Forty-fifth Street, and summers were spent at Oyster Bay, where a country home of their own, Sagamore Hill, where she would never live, was being planned.

Alice went into her ordeal cheerfully. She was not too well, but the doctors were suavely reassuring. There was a pleasant fluttering around the house on Fifty-seventh Street, where she spent much of her time while Theodore was at Albany. His sister Conie, who had become Mrs. Douglas Robinson, had a baby son, and the two young women had much in common. Alice enjoyed her new importance. She was playing the only vital part that a woman of her time could play—excepting, of course, the preposterous unsexed creatures who were beginning to talk about votes for women.

Roosevelt had been re-elected in 1882, and it would be necessary for him to campaign again in the fall of 1883. The star of his fame was rising rapidly. But he was tired. The work in the legislature was, "if conscientiously done, very harassing," and the 1884 session could be additionally so, since he was almost certain to become minority leader. Perhaps Roosevelt suffered, too, from a superfluity of feminine activity at home. Consequently, he decided to seek rec-

reation in the West and arrived at Little Missouri, in the Dakota Bad Lands, on the morning of September 7, 1883. Again, he had a delightful time, and it was signally fortunate that he had gone to the Bad Lands during that summer. Less than a year later, when in a single night his life changed utterly, he had a place of refuge. He was back in New York in time to conduct his campaign for the Assembly and was, as usual, returned without difficulty.

As the day of her confinement drew near, Roosevelt's young wife left the house on Forty-fifth Street to stay with her mother-in-law on Fifty-seventh, where an apartment was furnished for her on the third floor. She waited anxiously each week for Friday to arrive, when Theodore would return from Albany after the legislature had recessed for the week end.

The baby was expected about the middle of February, and life at the house on Fifty-seventh Street moved on with this uppermost. Alice was happy, if physically wretched. Only one trivial incident is remembered of those weeks of waiting: an afternoon when Alice and Mrs. Roosevelt were to go driving. A member of the family dropped by and found Alice sitting, the personification of patience, in the drawing room on the first floor. She was wearing furs, for it was cold outside. She laughed when asked why she was sitting there. The Little Motherling, she explained, using Theodore's pet name for his mother, was "always late, but not generally so late as this time."

February 13, 1884, was a Wednesday. On the previous Friday Corinne Robinson and her husband had gone to Baltimore, and before leaving Mrs. Robinson had jokingly told Alice that she must not have her baby until they returned. "I promise," she said cheerfully. Conie then said good-by to her mother, who was in bed with what seemed a mild indisposition. On Monday a telegram went to Baltimore stating that no need to hurry home had developed, and so Mr. and Mrs. Robinson delayed their return until Wednesday morning. Then, just before they took the train, there was good news. A girl had been born late on Tuesday night, February 12; the doctors said that Alice had survived the ordeal well. So the journey back to New York was made in high spirits. They reached New York on Wednesday evening, glad that the period of suspense was over and wondering whether Theodore had yet arrived from Albany. Details of reaching New York that evening, quite unnoticed at the time, always remained etched on the minds of Corinne Robinson and her husband. They remembered that fog hung over the Hudson River that night, and that the ferry which brought them from New Jersey was delayed because of it. They went uptown on an elevated railway train and, since there was no reason to hurry, walked from the station to the house. Seeing a light in the window on the third floor, Mrs. Robinson again gave thanks that the baby had been born and that Alice's suffering was behind her. Then she went up the steps. The door opened. Mrs. Robinson saw her brother Elliott standing in the doorway and knew from his face that something was wrong.

"If you want to see your baby," he said, "do so before you come into this house. He is over at your Aunt Gracie's. There is a curse on this house! Mother is dying, and Alice is dying, too."

It was then about 10:30. An hour later, Roosevelt came in, having been told only that a daughter had been born and having left the Assembly Chamber in the midst of effusive, good-natured congratulations. He found his wife barely able to recognize him, and all that night, save for one brief moment, he sat at the head of the bed and held her in his arms. Just before three o'clock in the morning his mother, who had developed typhoid fever, died, and Theodore, standing by her bed, echoed the words of his brother: "There *is* a curse on this house." Then he went back upstairs. Dawn dragged into the next day. At two o'clock on February 14, 1884, her body weakened by Bright's disease, Alice died. A year later Roosevelt wrote:

She was born at Chestnut Hill, Massachusetts, on July 29, 1861; I first saw her on October 18, 1878, and loved her as soon as I saw her sweet, fair young face; we were betrothed on January 25, 1880, and married on October 27th, of the same year; we spent three years of happiness such as rarely comes to man or woman; on February 12, 1884, her baby girl was born; she kissed it, and seemed perfectly well; some hours afterward she, not knowing that she was in the slightest danger, but thinking only that she was falling into a sleep, became insensible, and died at two o'clock on Thursday afternoon, February 14, 1884, at 6 West Fifty-seventh Street, in New York; she was buried two days afterward, in Greenwood Cemetery.

She was beautiful in face and form, and lovelier still in spirit; as a flower she grew, and as a fair young flower she died. Her life had been always in the sunshine; there had never come to her a single great sorrow; and none ever knew her who did not love and revere her for her bright, sunny temper and her saintly unselfishness. Fair, pure, and joyous as a maiden; loving, tender, and happy as a young wife; when she had just become a mother, when her life seemed to be but just begun, and when the years seemed so bright before her—then, by a strange and terrible fate, death came to her.

And when my heart's dearest died, the light went from my life forever.

On Saturday morning, February 16, two hearses moved side by side from the home on Fifty-seventh Street to the Fifth Avenue Presbyterian Church at Fifth Avenue and Fifty-fifth Street. Two rosewood coffins were carried in. The Reverend Dr. John Hall, who had been the family minister for years, could barely control himself as he made a brief address. One of the two women had done her work, he said, but the other was young. It seemed strange that she had been taken away. But Jesus was the Resurrection and the Life. Then he prayed for the husband and the little baby, three days old, and wept.

Theodore Roosevelt sat in a front pew, with Elliott Roosevelt, his father-in-law, and his sisters. The twin hearses moved again. The double interment was in Greenwood Cemetery.

Somehow, Roosevelt went on with his work; if proof were needed that he had courage and an iron will this fact alone would serve. . . . Then he fled to the quiet of the Bad Lands. At Albany, Assemblyman Hunt remembered, "you could not talk to him about it, you could see at once that it was a grief too deep. There was a sadness about his face that he never had before. He did not want anybody to sympathize with him. He hiked away to the wilderness to get away from the world. He went out there a broken-hearted man."

While he was in the West, Roosevelt wrote the memorial to his wife and mother, brief but deeply moving, which was printed in a limited edition and circulated among relatives and close friends. Roosevelt saw the relatives of his first wife whenever he was in Boston, and the daughter, who was to become Mrs. Nicholas Longworth, frequently visited them. But if Alice Lee, whom he met on that October day in 1878, was ever mentioned, there is no record of it. A door was closed on the three years they lived together, a door that was never opened. There is not a word in his autobiography to indicate that she had existed.

In time he may have doubted that she had. In December of 1886 he was married again, to the Edith Carow he had known as a child, and his married life was happy and complete. Five other children came. Four of them married and had children. One, the youngest, fell in an airplane behind the German lines. Honors came to Roosevelt; age came also. Only Alice Lee remains young and does not fade. She is forever fair; a figure on a Grecian urn.

Henry F. Pringle, formerly a distinguished New York newspaperman and professor of journalism at Columbia University, is now a contributor to several national magazines. This article, adapted from his Pulitzer Prize-winning Theodore Roosevelt: A Biography, *is used by permission of the author and Harcourt, Brace and Company, Inc.*

"Now defend yourself, you damned rascal!"

CONTINUED FROM PAGE 47

electoral votes. He lost the election to John Quincy Adams in the House of Representatives. From that point Benton was again Jackson's man and played a leading role in 1828, when Jackson became President.

Jackson's eight-year reign was a long succession of fierce political struggles involving personalities as often as principles. Old Hickory emerged as the champion of equality of opportunity in American life, opposed by the older economic aristocracy. In every battle Benton led the Jackson forces in the Senate.

The high point of Benton's personal devotion to Jackson followed a harsh Senate resolution charging Jackson with improper and unconstitutional conduct in removing government funds from the control of the Bank of the United States. Benton answered with a public avowal never to rest until the Senate should "expunge" the resolution from the official record.

For three years, in every session of Congress, he sang the President's praises and demanded his vindication, until the matter became a national issue. In 1836, when the Administration's followers finally won a clear-cut majority in the Senate, Benton launched the battle to clear Jackson's name.

Even with a majority, such a precedent-breaking action required careful planning. On the appointed day Benton prepared for a marathon session by stocking a committee room with "cold hams, turkeys, rounds of beef, pickles, wines, and cups of hot coffee." When opponents kept making speeches in hope of adjournment, the "expungers" were ready. As, with the passing hours, tempers began to wear, the delights of the banquet room were offered to the opposition; some accepted, but others haughtily refused. To Calhoun the expunging was a deed worthy of "Caligula and Nero"; to Clay, "like the blood-stained hands of the guilty Macbeth," it would never wash out; and to Webster it was a "ruthless violation of a sacred instrument." Webster, Clay, and Calhoun, and their many followers, had been bitterly humiliated by Jackson's victory over the Bank, and the expunging was the final rubbing of salt into raw, gaping wounds. By midnight the lobbies, the galleries, and the floor itself were jammed with excited people, and a few senators sent for arms to protect themselves from possible violence. Amid a mixture of cheers, groans, and hisses, the expunging resolution passed by a vote of 24 to 19.

The senatorial censure had been a sore spot for the tired old man in the White House, and this final victory over his most dedicated enemies was sweet. He assured Benton of "my high regard, and exalted opinion of your talents, virtue, and patriotism."

There was a final sequel. Senator Benton lived to write a history of his times, and the major theme of its huge first volume was the greatness of Andrew Jackson. If the making of a great man depends in part upon the historian, Benton made a significant contribution to Jackson's fame, because later scholars drew heavily upon Benton's work.

What was the importance of this friendship for the two men and their America? In 1812 Jackson's powerful enemies were eager to stifle his ambitions. The opportunity for the military fame which made Jackson President came because in a time of crisis Jackson had already mobilized an army which could not be ignored. The ideas and much of the work that went into creating this army came from recruiting officer Benton. An extensive poll of historians in 1948 judged Jackson to be one of America's six great Presidents because he planted his ideas and policies permanently in the life of America despite the most determined efforts of able and powerful opponents. And the victories supporting Jackson's claim to greatness usually found Benton leading the charge. Ironically enough, Benton's own career may have been furthered most by the quarrel and fight with Jackson because it caused his removal to the new frontier territory of Missouri, where the opportunities were greater and the competition less than in Tennessee.

The American people took Old Hickory Jackson and Old Bullion Benton to their hearts, indicating perhaps that they were truly representative of their America. Both men—by turns generous, kind, suspicious, openhearted, proud, gentle, jealous, violent, and tender—were capable of profound love and unrelenting hatred, the highest creativity and the most destructive ruthlessness. Occasionally disagreeable, they were never weak, cowardly, or dull. They sometimes personified the worst, but often the best, of young America in its great age of growing pains, and never more so than in their relations with one another.

Elbert B. Smith is a member of the faculty of Iowa State College. He gathered material for this article while doing research for Magnificent Missourian, *a biography of Thomas Hart Benton just published by J. B. Lippincott.*

Funston Captures Aguinaldo

CONTINUED FROM PAGE 29

his part magnificently without arousing any suspicion. Once across, the Little Macs formed ranks and marched up the bank to a point opposite Aguinaldo's guards. As the line swung abreast of the dictator's troops, Segovia called to his men and waved his hat. This was the signal, and in a moment eighty Mausers, Remingtons, and Krags barked a volley. Two guards went down, and the rest broke in confusion.

Still Aguinaldo did not surmise what had happened. Thinking that his men had fired a volley in honor of the new arrivals, he rushed to the window to order them to save their ammunition. As he did, Placido threw his arms about the dictator's waist and wrestled him to the ground, while Segovia dashed back into the room from the balcony where he had given the signal. Aguinaldo's officers began to recover from their shock and were drawing their side arms, when Segovia let fly with the six cartridges in his own revolver. He hit and downed two of the rebels; the rest surrendered or leaped out the windows and made for the river, where they escaped by swimming.

The rattle of rifle fire ended as swiftly as it had begun. Funston had reached the river just as the shooting commenced and crossed quickly. His timely intervention spared the lives of some of Aguinaldo's men who otherwise might have been killed by the aroused Macabebes. Inside the headquarters building Funston found the rebel commander helplessly pinned to the floor with the rotund Placido astride his back. It was only then that Aguinaldo realized what had happened and meekly surrendered.

The expedition was over, and Funston's men relaxed and dined luxuriously on the food left behind by the villagers, all of whom had fled to the hills at the first shot. On the morning of March 25, the party headed for Palanan Bay and the rendezvous with the *Vicksburg*.

On the way back to Manila Aguinaldo realized that the Americans intended him no violence, and he spoke to Funston quite frankly, admitting that he had been completely deceived by the letters. Within a few weeks he issued a proclamation from Manila urging his followers to lay down their arms and accept terms from the Americans. Except for a few pockets of resistance, the rebellion seemed broken.

General MacArthur recommended Funston for a general's star in the Regular Army. The hero was feted and lionized for his daring actions. Suddenly, however, it became evident that the approbation was not universal. In Washington a spirited debate broke out in the Senate over the confirmation of his new commission.

After considerable delay Funston's commission was confirmed in December 1901, and on January 9, 1902, he returned to America. But he was still the center of a violent controversy. Some anti-imperialists criticized anything or anyone connected with the American intervention in the Philippines. Others were genuinely shocked at the tactics Funston had used to capture Aguinaldo. He had, they charged, forged communications, clothed his men in enemy uniforms, accepted food from the man he planned to capture and gained admission to his stronghold by deception, and fired upon the guards without warning. All these constituted a damning indictment.

Never one to duck a fight, Funston countered with a speech in New York before the Lotos Club. He defended the Army and imperialism, and claimed that American lives were being lost because "misinformed and misguided" people at home were encouraging Filipino resistance.

When he went so far as to endorse hanging for critics of the war, Funston opened a breach between himself and his opponents that could not be closed. In the Senate Thomas M. Patterson of Colorado and Edward W. Carmack of Tennessee blistered him as "a Jayhawker Brigadier from the windswept plains, the mightiest Samson that ever wielded the jawbone of an ass as the weapon of war." Funston's violent diatribes against the senators proved embarrassing to the Administration, and on April 22, 1902, President Theodore Roosevelt ordered him to keep silent.

The controversy died down in time, and in 1906, when Funston commanded the troops in San Francisco after the great earthquake, he was universally praised as the man who saved that city from complete disaster.

Funston neither forgot nor forgave his critics, however, and some years later, while again stationed in the now-pacified Philippines, he remembered those who had criticized him for accepting food before capturing his benefactor. "I would be very much interested in seeing the results of a surgical operation performed on the skull of [such] a man," he wrote.

He reflected a moment longer on what such an operation would reveal, and then with his ever-sharp pen he wrote his answer: "Sweetbreads."

William F. Zornow, currently on leave from the faculty of Kansas State College, is the author of Kansas: A History of the Jayhawk State, *of* Lincoln and the Party Divided, **and of numerous magazine articles on historical subjects.**

READING, WRITING, AND HISTORY

By BRUCE CATTON

Morning Star

According to the legend, America is a nation devoted to pure action—a muscular, highly organized country, as little given to brooding introspection and as dedicated to physical activity as a professional football team. The simile may be a good one; we see to it, by elaborate mechanisms, that our colleges and universities provide an adequate, unfailing supply of skilled athletes and worry very little if the output of thinkers—physicists, let us say, or other eggheads—runs a trifle short of the potential demand. It may be that we live up to the legend a little too ardently.

Yet the legend itself is somewhat out of date. We *are* an introspective people, and we are becoming more so every day. The current revival of interest in American history is an indication of the fact.

There are a great many reasons for that revival, but one of the strongest, certainly, is an instinctive desire to make a correct appraisal of our present status. That status grows out of all of the yesterdays which are history's especial concern, and it is obviously something we want to examine as closely as we can. What are we like, as a people? What sort of civilization have we finally built up here? What has become of us, at last, after all of these historic alarms and excursions? What does our society mean today, and where have we finally got to?

This, perhaps, is what we are really looking for, as we at last elevate history into something tolerably popular and familiar. The only trouble is that none

of these plaintive questions can have a really satisfactory answer, because the simple truth is that we have not, so far, actually got anywhere yet—not anywhere that can serve as a place to pause and take a deep breath. History is a continuous process of change, and the change is still going on. We have not yet become something; we are still becoming. This bounteous year 1958 is no more the end of the journey than was 1861, or 1907, or any other year plucked at random from the calendar. New appraisals are all very well, but we Americans are still making our civilization, and what it will eventually look like is a secret.

So our introspection must be concerned chiefly with the attempt to get a line on that secret. We could hardly be better engaged, because even though we do

---

America as a Civilization: *Life and Thought in the United States Today,* by Max Lerner. Simon and Schuster. 1,036 pp. $10.00

---

not know just where we are going we are plainly going somewhere at a prodigious rate of speed, and unless we nourish a strong faith we are apt to wonder if the end of the journey may not be that steep place that leads down to the sea. To the examination of this secret Max Lerner applies himself diligently in a brooding, thoughtful new book aptly titled *America as a Civilization.*

We believe that we have a national tradition, says Mr. Lerner, but it is impossible to generalize about it very successfully because it is compounded of many subtraditions. We are the product of four separate waves of migration—the original movement of the Indians from Asia, the later movement of people from England and western Europe, the forced movement of the Negroes from Africa, and finally—what Mr. Lerner calls "the polyglot ethnic strain"—the great wave of all peoples from the Mediterranean, from central and eastern Europe, from Asia and from Latin America, and from everywhere else. Perhaps the one factor in common with the greatest of these waves was the pervading notion of America as a land of promise, a place where men could find well-being and freedom. America, in short, was built on a promise, and although we have been bothered ever since about the degree to which that promise has been fulfilled, the significant thing as Mr. Lerner sees it is the fact that the promise itself has always persisted. This is our great "social myth"; it has always pulled us on, and it always will, bringing abundant disillusionment but bringing also recurring triumphs of advance and achievement.

Along with this dominant myth there is another fact which Mr. Lerner considers unique to America. Alone among nations, he remarks, America has a history which "is also the history of the three shaping forces of the modern Western world"—industrialism as a technology, capitalism as a way of organizing it, and democracy as a way of running both. From these comes an immense dynamic force which moves hand in hand with the great motif of promise. Whatever we are becoming, then, it seems to Mr. Lerner highly likely that future historians will look back on our American life and see in it "one of the memorable civilizations of history."

All very well: and, specifically, how does this civilization seem to be taking shape? Mr. Lerner does not try to give any final, detailed answers; he simply looks about him, jots down some of the memorable images that are fastening themselves in our collective memories, and tries to arrive at a few very broad conclusions. Significantly, he finds that, even though we may be a less fluid people than we once were, we have not yet developed a single, well-defined "ruling class." We have an upper class, to be sure, a wealthy class, perhaps even a dominant class, but we do retain social mobility and the base of economic power is continually shifting. Rigidity has not yet set in.

Are we, with all of this, losing the drive and the sense of adventure that once (as we believe, anyway) characterized America? We are still a dynamic society, but we are becoming very security-conscious. Are we torn by a clash between these two emotional states, with the old urge to make new beginnings conflicting with the urge to reach a safe spot where risks need not

be taken? Possibly; for along with everything else Mr. Lerner concludes that "America is a happiness society even more than it is a freedom society or a power society." In our Declaration of Independence we asserted that one of man's inalienable rights is his right to pursue happiness, and we have been hard at the pursuit ever since, with varying degrees of success. Yet what else could come, in a land where the infinite promise of life is one of the traditional concepts? The pursuit of happiness is not a bad thing, once we understand just what happiness is and how it may best be attained.

We are no longer an isolated country, cut off from the rest of the world by broad oceans. Whether we like it or not, we are now one of the world's two great powers, and what we are and do—whether we are at our best or our worst—touches the imagination of the rest of mankind in a way (as Mr. Lerner suggests) that only one other society, the Roman Empire, ever touched it. The parallel is disquieting, perhaps; for the Romans themselves lost their own imagination, they came to value things more than they valued ideas, and the end was darkness. Will that be our destiny as a civilization? This grim question lies at the end of all our introspection.

To this question Mr. Lerner does not pretend to have a final answer. Any thoughtful student of American life can see many reasons for bleak pessimism, and as a highly perceptive man Mr. Lerner sees them as clearly as anyone needs to. But he retains his optimism—largely, it would seem, because our society is still in this process of becoming. The great enemy of any civilization, he suggests, is "the enemy within," which is simply rigidity. That has not yet come to us. We are still developing; our sources of creativeness have not gone dry. At the end of his long survey, Mr. Lerner is able to say, with Emerson: "We think our civilization is near its meridian, but we are yet only at the cock crowing and the morning star."

Go It Alone

This exercise in considering our society as a world civilization is a useful one, but it does run counter to a powerful, deeply embedded impulse in American life—the impulse to look on America as a land set apart from all others, able to go its own way without reference to what the rest of the world may be doing. The man who is ruled by this impulse we call an isolationist, and when we try to appraise what we are and where we are going he is one of the people we need to examine. Who is he, and just how did he get that way?

An excellent study is now available in a book called *The Isolationist Impulse*, written by Selig Adler, professor of history at the University of Buffalo. Mr. Adler begins his inquiry by pointing out that it is necessary first of all to define isolationism correctly. American isolationism, he remarks, "has never meant total social, cultural and economic self-sufficiency." Few Americans have ever believed in that, and the whole course of American history is against it. We have always exchanged both goods and ideas with the rest of the world, and we have never even dreamed of the iron-walled retreat into a hermit's life similar to that of the Japan of the shoguns. American isolationism is simply a determination to stay out of foreign wars, coupled with an unwavering refusal to enter into alliances; a belief that we must always go it alone. Isolationists, says Mr. Adler, "cling tenaciously to faith in the unchangeability of our changing world."

This, to be sure, is where the shoe pinches, because the world is changing very radically, and some of the change comes from what we ourselves do. Yet the drive to go it alone is strong and it has deep roots in the American past, and Mr. Adler is concerned with getting these roots out and seeing what they amount to.

This inquiry leads him into a study of American history since, roughly, the time of the First World War. We got into a war which we had supposed we could stay out of, we oversold ourselves (once we got in) on what was going to be accomplished, and at the end it seemed that all of our fine hopes had been blighted. It was precisely then that the isolationist impulse came to full flower, and it proved an extremely hardy

---

The Isolationist Impulse: *Its Twentieth-Century Reaction*, by Selig Adler. Abelard-Schuman, Ltd. 538 pp. $6.75.

---

growth; bruised and trodden on though it has been of late, it is a long way from being dead. Where did it get its strength?

Step by step, Mr. Adler traces it. Woodrow Wilson ran into many difficulties, some of them self-created, when he came back from Paris with the draft Treaty of Versailles and the concept of a League of Nations. The liberals, previously among his strong supporters, fell away from him. The pro-league arguments were cast in an unreal, idealistic form, instead of being based on the obvious point that it was to our material interest to set up machinery that would curb aggression and war; and in 1919 America had grown very disillusioned about idealism. The election of 1920 was tragically misinterpreted; everyone assumed that it was a referendum on the treaty and on the league, when in fact (as Mr. Adler insists) it was the result of the

interaction of many very complex forces, including simple war-weariness. Not for years thereafter would any political party be willing to go to the people with an internationalist program.

Then came the Harding Administration, in which, as Mr. Adler says, we tried to retain the benefits of isolationism and still reap the benefits of a privileged position in the world's market places. Washington washed its hands of responsibility for world economic conditions just when big business was getting into world economic affairs up to both elbows. Our statesmen and industrialists, imagining themselves perfectly in tune with each other, went in diametrically opposite directions.

The world economic depression—which, at least in part, grew out of this—greatly intensified the desire for isolation; and, as Mr. Adler says, "the isolationism of the 1930's was much more profound than the rather superficial detachment of the preceding decade." Dabbling in European affairs, apparently, had not only cost us our ideals but a great deal of money as well. We withdrew further into ourselves; at which moment came a new wave of aggressions, overseas, which tended to confirm our deep suspicions that international politics was no game for us. The New Deal did not stem the tide. On the contrary, the high-water mark of isolationism came in the neutrality legislation which bloomed between 1935 and 1937. Ironically, this legislation, Mr. Adler believes, made war all the more likely, for it helped persuade the megalomaniac Axis leaders that "the United States would stand by as they tore up the maps of Europe and Asia."

Out of all this came, at last, the Second World War, which reversed the trend. It was not followed by a general retreat of the liberals, as had been the case in 1919, and it clearly destroyed the isolationist argument that if we fought against Fascism we would destroy the very values we were trying to save. Also, on a purely material plane, it restored the pulsing prosperity which had been missing for more than a decade. We no longer wanted to get back to a happier prewar age, because the prewar age, this time, did not look worth regaining. There was an aftermath, to be sure, and the postwar witch hunts can be seen as a final flare-up of the isolationist mood, but the great drive was over.

Over—for keeps? Mr. Adler is not entirely certain. We have not yet found, he sagely remarks, an adequate substitute for isolationism. The collective security ideal is still in the blueprint stage, the international situation is (to say the least) unpromising, and there could still be a revival of the insular tradition. We have always been torn between a desire to use our power to stabilize the world and an urge to remain aloof. At the moment the internationalists seem to have won; but their victory, Mr. Adler warns, was "a decision rather than a knockout." The isolationists may yet demand a rematch; meanwhile, "the only certain thing about the future is its uncertainty."

What We Are Like

Civilization, in the nature of things, is an experiment, and the test of its excellence (failing a better one) is probably its capacity for survival. The chief difference between our civilization and others may be that from the beginning ours has been a conscious experiment; at every step we have been pragmatists, shooting the works on the chance that what we were up to would somehow bring in the blue chips.

This, in any case, is the suggestion advanced by Bradford Smith in a light, entertaining, and frequently very perceptive book entitled *Why We Behave Like Americans*. In a way Mr. Smith (who was assisted in this book by Marion Collins Smith) is covering the same field Mr. Lerner plowed so assiduously; he is doing it with less gravity and in less space, and his book makes an excellent companion volume.

We have been trying new things in this country, says Mr. Smith, ever since the Pilgrim fathers were told by the Indians that it would be a good idea to drop a rather dead fish in every corn hill to fertilize it, after which it would be every man for himself. The fathers tried it, it worked, and since then we have been receptive to new ideas, some of which panned out properly.

But although we know a great deal about ourselves, we do not necessarily understand too much; and Mr. Smith's book is an essay directed toward a broader understanding. Understanding, he believes, grows out of a knowledge of all of the things that go to shape a culture—physical environment, human influences, institutions, artistic expressions, and the way in which the people involved go about making a living, reproducing their kind, and expressing their inner yearnings. His book, accordingly, is directed (without too much solemnity) toward an examination of all of these aspects of American society, and it is highly readable.

There are, as Kipling once remarked, many different ways of constructing tribal lays, and all of them are right. Mr. Lerner's way is solemn and thorough; Mr. Smith's is light and occasionally irreverent. As a sample, in his discussion of the American character, he expresses himself thus:

"Americans are a peculiar people. They work like mad, then give away much of what they earn. They play until they are exhausted, and call this a vacation.

They love to think of themselves as tough-minded business men, yet they are push-overs for any hard luck story. They have the biggest of nearly everything including government, motor cars and debts, yet they are afraid of bigness. They are always trying to chip away at big government, big business, big unions, big influence. They like to think of themselves as little people, average men, and they would like to cut everything down to their own size. Yet they boast of their tall buildings, high mountains, long rivers, big meals. Theirs is the best family, the best neighborhood, the best state, the best country, the best world, the best heaven. They also have the most traffic deaths, the most waste, the most racketeering."

Well, so far, so good; and it is fairly easy to go on in this vein, so long as you are not required to touch base anywhere. Mr. Smith does touch base; that is, he can think hard while writing easily (not too simple a trick), and he does a really good job of describing the way in which the American spirit expresses itself. It does so, he seems to feel, on a largely informal basis. Every crisis in American history finds people doing some of their biggest jobs through wholly voluntary associations—as via the Sons of Liberty, in the days

---

Why We Behave Like Americans, by Bradford Smith, assisted by Marion Collins Smith. The J. B. Lippincott Co. 322 pp. $4.95.

---

when a great ferment of libertarian ideas was leading up to the American Revolution; as in the case of the Underground Railroad, which did so much to put the skids under slavery. The point is that Americans always want to remain free private citizens and individuals, but they do realize that they are bound to the community and must exert their influence upon it. They advance democracy not so much through politics as through an *ad hoc* system of working together on their own hook. We are rugged individualists, but we always recognize that we belong to the group.

So Mr. Smith goes on, sketching in briefly all manner of facets of American life, from public schools to newspapers and from political caucuses to trade associations and the conventions of fraternal organizations. He comes to no more positive final conclusions than Mr. Lerner reaches; like him, he does manage to complete his survey with a feeling of hope—the result of an appraisal of a society which draws vitality and optimism from its youth and its abundance. And like him, too, he has the sense of a nation which has not yet "arrived" but which is still working its way—blindly, and often with great waste and error, but always with energy—through its perplexing but promising formative stages.

The Social Structure of Early Massachusetts

By GILMAN M. OSTRANDER

Settlers of Massachusetts
Were of two sets:
Those by Grace of God elected;
Those rejected.

One good way to tell the sainted
From the tainted
Was that those whose prayers were heeded
Had succeeded.

As a rule it therefore followed
That the hallowed
Were the favored upper classes,
Not the masses.

Quite a number of the lowly
Acted holy,
Hoping they had been elected
Unsuspected.

Others reasoned, after learning
Hell-fire burning
Was to be their fate forever,
—Now or never.

They were common people which is
Why so many turned out witches.

RICHARD ERDOES